Drawing
and
Painting
the
FIGURE

Drawing
and
Painting
the
FIGURE

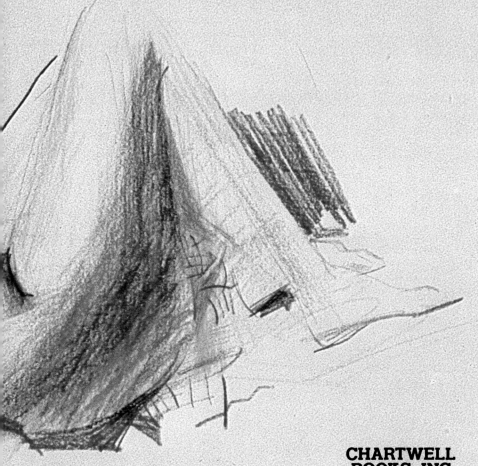

**CHARTWELL
BOOKS, INC.**

symbolism, particularly in the use of color. Figures were set against areas of flat color, often gold or blue, or sometimes a richly elaborated pattern of jewel-like shapes.

In Byzantium, the capital of what had been the Eastern or Greek-speaking part of the Roman Empire, pictures which represented Christ, his mother Mary or the saints, came to be considered holy in themselves. Artists were strictly required to paint within traditionally acceptable guidelines; only certain ways of depicting the figure, facial expressions and gestures were permitted. A typical Byzantine altar-painting, *Enthroned Madonna and Child*, demonstrates both the restrictions imposed by the Church and a touch of the realism from earlier times. The figure is seated on a throne placed against a

Above *Madonna Enthroned*, Giotto. Rejecting the stylized art of Byzantine and contemporary Sienese painters, Giotto attempted to render a more naturalistic world and is thus regarded as a founder of modern painting. By simplifying the drapery, he makes the figure stand out as a solid mass, and by using green pigment as an undercoat, achieves relief on the two-dimensional plane. Although posed similarly to the Byzantine Madonna, the solid, massive frame of Giotto's sculptural Madonna has a humanity and naturalism which was the major part of Giotto's contribution to art.

Above *The Trinity* (c.1426), Masaccio. Masaccio's style is akin to Giotto's in its realism, narrative power and the way in which he creates space, light and solidity of form. His naturalism owes much to the architect Brunelleschi, the pioneer of the central perspective system and is shown clearly in this fresco in Santa Maria Novella, in Florence. Concerned more with the underlying structure of objects than with surface decoration, Masaccio uses light to define the construction of a body and its draperies. Set within a perspectively created space, which gives the impression of actually being a chapel extension, the figures stand with the light falling on their volumetric drapery assuring the solidity of their forms. Christ's body demonstrates Masaccio's knowledge of anatomy, derived from a study of classical sculpture. A humanist and intellectual art, it results in monumental and austere forms perfectly in accord with the scientific aims of the Renaissance.

Above right *Sacred and Profane Love* (c.1516), Titian. Painted to celebrate the marriage of Niccolò Aurelio, a Venetian humanist and collector, the subject of the painting was chosen from neo-Platonic writings. The nude figure, unashamedly displaying her beautiful, voluptuous body, represents the principle of universal and eternal love while the richly dressed figure, possibly a portrait of the bride, stands for natural love. Titian uses large planes of brilliant blue, red, rose and green to set off the sculptural forms whose warm flesh tones and generous proportions contrast with the hard outlines of the sarcophagus, making them two of the most beautiful female figures in Renaissance art.

Right *Perspective study* (c.1480), Leonardo da Vinci. In this pen and ink preparatory study simply for the background of his *Adoration of the Magi*, Leonardo has used the central point perspective propounded by Brunelleschi. Perspective plots a stage in which to place figures in correct spatial relationships but also has a dynamic quality – note the vanishing point is to the right of center, matching the vigor of the figural movements. The rearing horsemen announce Leonardo's lifelong interest in this extremely difficult anatomical subject.

flat, gold background. Although the composition has an abstract quality and is treated as a pattern of flat shapes, the line representing the back of the throne which encircles the Madonna nevertheless implies an enclosed space and therefore depth. Again, the folds of the Madonna's robes are highly stylized in the way they fall from her shoulders, around her arms and over her knees, but they give a good impression of the shape underneath, including a foreshortening of the upper legs. The expression on the faces of both mother and child is serene, though solemn, a reminder of the religious fervour that permeates Byzantine art. The human figure was always portrayed in certain rigid poses which the artists learnt as apprentices. Anything not included in this repertoire would have been difficult to represent as no one ever drew directly from the figure – there seems to have been neither the demand nor the need.

Nearly all the surviving paintings from this time are of religious scenes, but this does not necessarily imply that no other paintings were produced. Private homes, castles and palaces probably contained non-religious paintings, but these were vulnerable to the whims of private owners whereas paintings in churches were revered and protected. It is difficult to judge whether artists obeyed the same set of rules when producing secular pieces, but it seems probable. The artist had again become an artisan, trained in a skilled craft but not expected to be innovative. Painting was often considered an adjunct to architecture at this time. Even when a painting was not made directly on the wall of a church or cathedral, its size was designed specifically for the proposed location, so imposing further constraints on an already rigidly ordered style of painting.

The work of Giotto di Bondone (c. 1267 - 1337) is generally recognized to have been a major turning point. His paintings may still appear static to modern eyes, but when compared with the work of his contemporaries it can easily be seen that Giotto was breaking the pattern. His treatment of form has a monumental quality not apparent in other paintings of the time, in spite of the backgrounds which at first remained flat, in the current style. The Ognissanti *Madonna*, painted by Giotto in about 1308, still retains much of the Gothic mood; it has a typically symmetrical composition with the Madonna seated centrally on a throne, surrounded by saints and angels. However the figures, especially those of Mary and Jesus, appear sculptured because the artist made effective use of tone. Mother and child are posed in almost exactly the same way as the Byzantine *Enthroned Madonna*, but the folds of drapery which had, until then, been set into a standardized pattern are transformed by Giotto into rich, flowing lines. The faces, though still serene, look capable of changing their expressions, and the babe's proportions are less like those of a miniature adult.

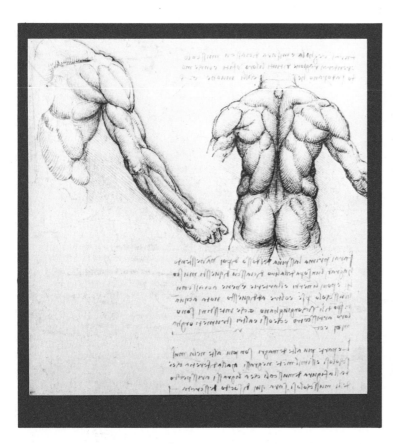

Above *Study of a Male Torso,* Leonardo da Vinci. Leonardo's notebooks were filled with studies of birds, cloud formations, water effects, skeletons, flowers and children in the womb. These minutely detailed sketches show his preoccupation with a scientific rendition of musculature, utilized in his interest in displaying the figure in movement.

Giotto's work was obviously considered valuable and unusual during his lifetime. It is known that he was greatly admired by Dante. Some of Giotto's finest work is contained within the Arena Chapel at Padua in northern Italy. This is an architecturally undistinguished chapel which was, unusually, built specifically to house these 36 fresco paintings, illustrating the lives of Christ and the Virgin. Giotto was painting not simply events, but moods, feelings and emotions; it is this which marks him out as an innovator.

It took some time for these new ideas to have any effect. The next half-century saw a general loosening of style, with artists increasingly interested in the use of light and shade and beginning, like Giotto, to represent their figures as human beings with human emotions. Coming at the tail end of an era which had devoted much of its creative spirit to religious fervor, these awakening techniques and the idea that artistic subjects could be other than divine, were revelations to artists and philosophers alike. The emphasis in figure painting was changing from religion toward realism, from the artist as instrument to the artist as creator. Available materials and pigments were simultaneously improving, and canvas was introduced as a support, releasing artists from medieval conventions into a greater freedom.

Above *Arnolfini and his Wife,* (1434), Jan van Eyck. Van Eyck is the major artist of the Early Netherlandish school. Among his achievements was the perfection of an oil medium and varnish fluid enough for him to obtain extremely subtle light effects and minute detail. This enabled him to create an extraordinary realism through the depiction of contrasting textures, space and light. Although the pose of Arnolfini and his wife is still medieval, the shadow on the somber faces, the attention to detail in the rich furs and materials, and the light

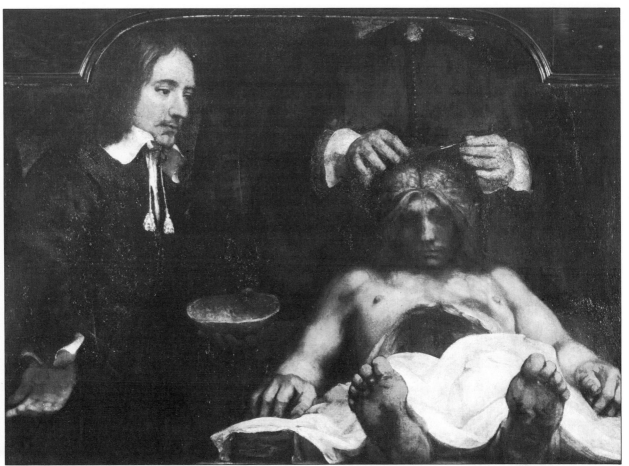

In the early fifteenth century, a discovery was made by a young architect which was to prove an inspiration to contemporaries and to succeeding generations. Filippo Brunelleschi (1377-1446) revealed what is now known as "the single vanishing point". The Romans had been aware of perspective and had made use of it in a limited way, but they had never understood the principles. Having established that there must be a fixed eye level, Brunelleschi found that lines running away from the viewer into the picture, although they are parallel, appear to converge to a single vanishing point on the eye level. Geometrical harmony and mathematics, so beloved by Classical artists, were to come into their own once more, to create the illusion of depth.

Masaccio (1401-28) was one of the first to realize the extent to which perspective could be used to imply space and depth. He used architectural detailing in his painting of *The Trinity* to place the figures within an alcove in the wall. A later artist, Uccello (1397 - 1475), was so excited by perspective that he worked ceaselessly in his experiments to establish the principles and mathematical rules by which it worked. His famous *Battle of San Romano* consists of three panels in which he has constructed a grid made up of fallen lances and figures to create an illusion of depth within the picture plane. In spite of his vigorous application of the rules which he had worked out, Uccello made mistakes. A fallen figure in the foreground, although painstakingly foreshortened, is out of scale with its surroundings and the overall effect of the painting is unreal and disjointed. Piero della Francesca (1410/20 - 1492), who was slightly younger than Uccello, had a better grasp of the atmospheric quality of perspective and was able to suggest depth not just by diminishing size but by decreasing tonal contrast. Whereas Uccello's figures are like well-made models in a stage setting, Piero's are real people in real locations. Often they were modeled on local dignitaries who were flattered to have their portraits included in religious paintings.

The Renaissance was a period of upheaval because it marked a change from the common belief in a divine order to a greater understanding of the scientific rules which govern the universe. Principles about proportion and the anatomy, solid form, space and depth, initially made by the Greeks, were

coming in from the window belong to the scientific age. Reflected in the mirror behind in remarkable perspective are the back views of his patrons and facing out, the artist himself.

Above *The Anatomy Lesson* (1656); Rembrandt van Rijn. Rembrandt first made his name with a painting of *The Anatomy Lesson of Doctor Tulp* in 1632. This painting was also commissioned for the anatomical theater of Amsterdam and depicts its lecturer, Doctor Deyman, dissecting the brain. It is a calculated design, the central figure which is nude and frontal, and steeply foreshortened, harking back to the perspective of Renaissance art theory. Rembrandt may have been influenced by Mantegna's *Dead Christ*. The strong *chiaroscuro* emphasizes the pathos of the scene, and illuminates the gory brain area and excavated stomach; the assistant on the left holds the removed skull. The painting illustrates the seventeenth-century fascination with science and medicine and Rembrandt's own particular interest in anatomy. Operations like this were often carried out on condemned men.

21

rediscovered. These new lines of thought are nowhere more evident than in the visual arts. However, they were not without opposition. Savonarola (1452 - 1498), a fanatical preacher of doom in the fifteenth century who feared the moral results of scientific progress, persuaded Sandro Botticelli (1445-1510) to burn bundles of his drawings, many of which demonstrated the new learning.

During the Renaissance, artists became less dependent upon the Church for patronage because of the rise of rich families who were able to encourage the arts and, incidentally, record their ascent to power. There was a reemergence of portrait painting which was to surpass even the achievements of the Roman period. Giovanni di Arrigo Arnolfini was an Italian merchant based in Bruges who wished to document his marriage to Jeanne de Chenany, set in a comfortable, affluent background which epitomized contemporary bourgeois luxury. The double portrait of *Arnolfini and his Wife* by Jan van Eyck (doc. 1422-d.1441) who painted it for their marriage in 1434, is an excellent example of the way in which secular painting still retained much of the influence of medieval

Top *Venus and Cupid* (*c.*1560), Titian. The Holy Roman Emperor, Charles V, was one of Titian's most eager patrons, commissioning paintings on religious and imperial themes, and a series of erotic subjects, known as *poesie*, mythological in title and blatantly erotic in content. This late painting shows a full-blown, heavy figure, the loosely handled paint and sensitive merging of autumnal colors creating a sense of warmth and shimmering light into which form is dissolved.

Above *Jupiter and Antiope* (*c.*1532), Correggio. Correggio painted several pictures for private patrons with classical subject matter having strongly erotic overtones. One of four compositions depicting Jupiter's amours, this scene shows Antiope's marvellously soft, languorous body, its soft warm tones set against the dark greens and browns as Jupiter takes her by surprise.

Right *L'Odalisca*, François Boucher. Correggio's sensual compositions look forward to Boucher's Rococo style. Boucher painted numerous mythological pictures in which the subject was transformed into wittily indelicate *scènes galantes,* full of light-hearted voluptuousness.

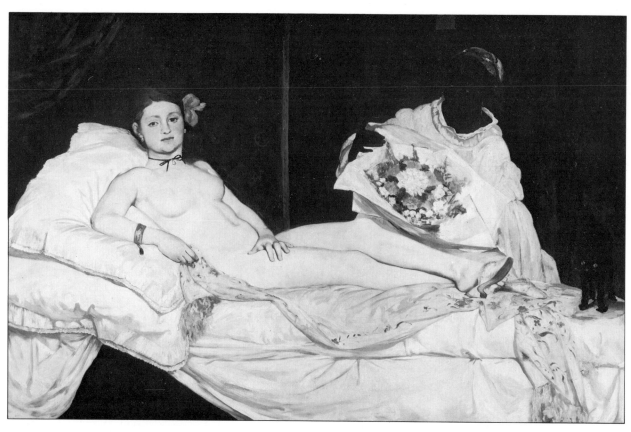

Above *Olympia* (1863), Edouard Manet. Rebelling against the academic history painting prevalent in France in his youth, Manet created a new style based on Velasquez, Goya and Ribera (1591-1652) in which he used the opposition of light and shadow with very little half-tone, a restricted palette with an emphasis on black, and painted directly from the model. His paintings caused much indignation, particularly the *Déjeuner sur l'Herbe* which closed the 1863 Salon and *Olympia*, exhibited in 1865. A Realist painter, he portrayed the world around him, sometimes with surprising touches. By placing the bed and body against a dark background, and throwing direct light with very little shadow on the forms, Olympia's cool sexuality directly addresses the spectator, her carefully placed hand drawing attention to what it pretends to hide.

symbolism, while utilizing recent discoveries and innovations. The artist was aware of the rules of perspective recently discovered and utilized in Italy, and his painting is a good demonstration of how quickly new thinking was spread through the civilized world.

Released from the strict confines of religious painting, artists were free to use a wider range of subjects and there was a resurgence of interest in mythological themes. Also, the study of anatomy, abandoned for centuries, was resumed with vigor, leading to a mastery of nude painting in this period. Once the rules of perspective had paved the way to a greater realism, it was natural that artists should become interested not just in the outward appearance of the human body but also in its underlying structure. The sketchbooks of Leonardo da Vinci show that he had made a study of anatomy, including a careful dissection of corpses which was considered almost blasphemous at the time. His exploratory drawings include the investigation of the growth of a child in the womb, and numerous annotated studies of parts of the body.

The Renaissance curiosity was not confined to the visual arts but was also concerned with philosophy and science. The body was studied for its own sake, not just for the sake of realism in art. Artists were required to record facts and results; their role

changed in this sphere, by necessity. Leonardo recorded his own discoveries; Rembrandt (1606-69), in 1632, recorded the mood of scientific curiosity in his first major group portrait, *The Anatomy Lesson of Dr Tulp*. He returned to this theme in 1656, when he painted *The Anatomical Lesson of Dr Joan Deyman*, which depicts the dissection of the human brain.

With the growing interest in and understanding of the naked body, combined with fewer moral constraints, asceticism gave way to sensuality, at first tentatively, and later with wholehearted delight. Patrons encouraged artists to produce works with only a thinly veiled erotic content. The paintings of Titian (*c.* 1487-1576), Correggio (*c.* 1489-1534), Rubens and Boucher (1703-70) are examples of a frank enjoyment of voluptuous female flesh. Oil paint came to be increasingly widely used, and the laying of transparent glazes, one on top of the other, allowed artists to paint with a transparency and luminosity that lent itself well to a sympathetic rendering of flesh, and, at the same time, to blend tones which created a great vitality.

A fascination with the texture and elasticity of skin and its light-reflecting qualities was constant through the next few centuries. The eighteenth and nineteenth centuries saw some of the most sensitive and sensual painting of the female nude, but

Left *Diana,* Auguste Renoir. A French Impressionist painter, Renoir's paintings have elements of the decorative techniques of the eighteenth century and Boucher's pretty color. He introduced the "rainbow palette" into the Impressionist technique which was restricted to pure tone and eliminated black. The human figure, especially female, formed a more important part of his art than in that of his fellow painters, and there are many studies of charming women, young girls, flowers and pretty scenes. His late works are mainly nudes, fleshy and voluptuous, the warm, pink skin tones enabling him to use his favorite color scheme of pinks. and reds. "It is necessary," he said "to be able to actually *feel* the buttocks and breasts."

there was a danger of the subject becoming stifled by the classical tradition many artists sought to emulate. There was a strange double standard which accepted paintings of nude figures in a classical mold as respectable but cried out in horror at work which simply presented the body as a thing of beauty, worth revealing simply for its own sake. It is ironic that this same attitude was the basis of most of the work produced in Ancient Rome, when female nudes were presented in mythological settings. The attitude is pinpointed by Auguste Renoir (1841-1919), when he described a nude painting "which was considered pretty improper, so I put a bow in her hand and a deer at her feet. I added the skin of an animal to make her nakedness less blatant – and the picture became a Diana."

It was no doubt this sort of hypocrisy which prompted Edouard Manet (1832-83) to paint his notorious *Déjeuner sur l'Herbe,* which, despite being based on *The Judgement of Paris* by Raphael (1483-1520), caused a huge public outcry when it was exhibited because of the juxtaposition of the naked woman with the fully clothed men. The fact that the nude is relaxed in the woodland scene and the men seem like intruders in spite of their obvious pleasure, enhances the absurdity of convention. Two years later, in 1865, Manet painted *Olympia* which was received with shock and outrage. In this painting the viewer finds his gaze returned with disconcerting candor by a nude who is reclining on a bed draped with splendidly decadent silks and tassels.

Toward the end of the nineteenth century, artists began to create works in which the nude figure is painted performing everyday tasks. Edgar Degas (1834-1917) and Pierre Bonnard (1867-1947) both produced a number of pictures of women in the bathtub, combing their hair and so on, which are like intimate glimpses into the subject's private life. At the same time as the content was becoming less important in the new freedom, the way it was treated was gaining importance. The Impressionists, for instance, were preoccupied with light and color being reflected or partially absorbed by objects and wanted to convey the effects of light in the paint. The Fauves were concerned to portray emotion using particularly strong colors.

The choice of subject matter in painting is now relatively free of convention, if not of inhibition. It is interesting, however, that representing the male nude is still frowned on, although it is legally and morally permissible. Artists can today concentrate on the methods and techniques of representing the human figure, with a firm backup of scientific knowledge, and need not be concerned about society's reaction.

Above *The Tub*, Edgar Degas.
Degas has used pure pastel,
strong colors and a simple
composition for this drawing.
The strokes sometimes move
across the body and sometimes
with it, a technique which
imbues the work with life.
Far left *La Gommeuse et les
Cercleux*, Jean Louis Forain
(1852-1939). Form and mood is
brilliantly suggested by light
falling on the men's faces and
shirt-fronts and highlighting the
scantily dressed girl.
Left *The Night* (1918-19), Max
Beckmann (1884-1950). A
leading German Expressionist,
Beckmann painted several
allegories reflecting the human
condition. The brutal, cruel
figures are depicted in a semi-
Cubist style, evoking a
nightmarish world in a fusion of
dream and reality.
Right *The Kiss*, Gustav Klimt.
Klimt has created one body out
of two, swathing the two lovers
in a stylized cloak, and achieving
a highly decorative effect.

THE ANATOMY

Early Anatomical Research

Teaching in art schools has always included a strong emphasis on figure drawing and drawing from life. The body is a complex piece of machinery; making convincing visual representation of it requires an understanding which can only be gained by detailed preliminary study. Today, this is greatly facilitated by the wealth of anatomical and physiological information readily available to the art student in libraries, but this has not always been the case. There was, for a long time, a reluctance to use the dead body for anatomical dissection and much "knowledge" was simply guesswork. The instinctive horror which caused people to recoil from dismembering a corpse was usually bound up in religious beliefs and a considerable fear of the unknown. Early Christians, for example, suspected that after the soul had left the body, it continued to hover for a while in close proximity. The combination of respect and fear led to a widely held opinion that the violation of mortal remains was morally wrong. These factors inhibited a scientific study of the human anatomy until well into the Enlightenment of the eighteenth century.

Artists from Ancient Greece and Rome arrived at their understanding of the human anatomy largely through surface study, which makes the level of their attainment remarkable. The word "anatomy" was invented by the Greeks, who made great advances in understanding the structure and functions of various parts of the body, but their findings were not always accurate. In spite of the teachings of Socrates (469-399 B.C.) and his pupil Plato (c. 427-347 B.C.) on the unimportance of the body after death, actual dissection of the human corpse was severely limited out of respect for mortal remains. Early anatomists conducted much of their research on animals, with the result that they made some fundamental errors of judgement.

The first anatomical studies of any authority were carried out around 300 B.C. by Erasistratus and Herophilus of the Ptolemaic medical school in Alexandria, who were later accused, probably without justification, of human vivisection. Although it is certain that they conducted a number of dissections, possibly even some in public, and that their studies were to be an important source of information for following generations, this type of inquiry was to cease with their death and was not seriously revived for more than 1,000 years.

Because of the moral climate in which these early dissections took place, there is little satisfactory documentary evidence about them. The writings of Galen (c. A.D. 130 – c. 200) in the second century A.D. are largely based upon the dissection of monkeys and apes, although his book *Bones for Beginners* was the result of seeing a human skeleton in the medical school in Alexandria. References to the subject over the next few centuries indicate that human dissection was discouraged, if not actually forbidden on religious grounds.

It is not until the thirteenth century that there is evidence of official lessons in anatomy taking place. In Salerno, Italy, it was decreed that the study of anatomy should be an obligatory part of a surgeon's training and there are records of post-mortems and autopsies being carried out in the medical faculty of the University of Bologna. By the beginning of the fourteenth century the practice of human dissection was common

Below Mondino de Luzzi is considered by many to have been the first professor of anatomy, working in the University of Bologna during the early part of the fourteenth century. This picture depicts Luzzi directing a dissection, and was used as the frontispiece of the 1493 edition of his book *Anathomia*. Luzzi's book and his teachings were heavily influenced by the often inaccurate work of Galen, and, while professors conducted their research and teachings from high pedestals, only allowing assistants to touch the body, no real progress was made in anatomical research.

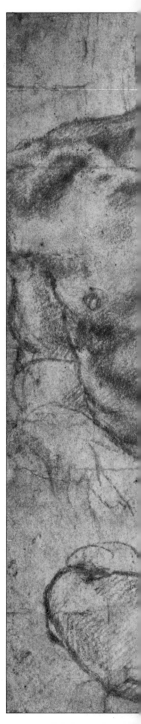

Above A study for *The Creation of Adam*, Michelangelo. This figure was to be used in a section of the Sistine Chapel fresco in Rome, which was painted between 1508 and 1512. Michelangelo considered himself to be primarily a sculptor, and this is apparent from his treatment of the figure. The accurate representation of the positions and interrelations of the bones and muscles of the male torso is drawn with force and vigor and shaded with great subtlety to give a powerful, almost monumental statement of volume. There is also great emotive force in the pose; although the figure is reclining, leaning back on his elbow, the reaching movement of the left arm provides a tension which implies that the body is communicating with another, even if the viewer is unaware of the whole picture. Adam's feelings of innocent love and acceptance are obvious in the position of the body; the facial expression hardly needs to be seen.

across Europe, including England. Although the subjects of these dissections were usually the bodies of executed criminals, the supply cannot have been too plentiful as there were many instances of grave-robbing by over-enthusiastic medical students.

As rules relaxed concerning dissections, it became customary for medical schools to give public demonstrations which were well attended. They were directed by a professor who did not touch the body but indicated where cuts should be made by pointing with a stick. The person who in fact wielded the knife would be a barber or servant with little social status who simply carried out orders.

It was natural that artists should become closely involved in the progress which was being made in the medical field. Apart from their own curiosity, which combined with their aim of truly representing the human figure, they were needed to document developments and provide illustrations for books of instruction on the subject. All such records, which would now be made with the camera, relied upon the skill and accurate observation of painters and draftsmen. Leonardo da Vinci, who carried out dissections for his own information, and made hundreds of carefully observed drawings of each stage, wrote in one of his notebooks: "I have dissected more than ten human bodies, destroying all the various members and removing the minutest particles of flesh which surrounded the veins, without causing any effusion of blood other than the imperceptible bleeding of the capillary veins. And as one single body did not suffice for so long a time, it was necessary to proceed by stages with so many bodies as would render my knowledge complete". He described the artistic reasons for such an investigation in these direct terms: "Perhaps you may lack the skill in drawing, essential for such representation, and if you had the skill in drawing, it may not be combined with a knowledge of perspective; and if it is so combined you may not understand the method of geometrical demonstration and the methods of estimating the force and strength of muscles; or perhaps you may be wanting in patience so that you will not be diligent".

Leonardo was in no doubt about his contribution to medical science, and his studies of anatomy and of physiology have been proved to be of lasting importance to medical and art students alike. He was not

Right One of a great number of illustrations in *De Humanis Corporis Fabrica* by Vesalius (1514-1564), this displays the underlayers of muscles. Vesalius completed the intricately researched and detailed tomes in 1543, rousing the fury of contemporary academics.

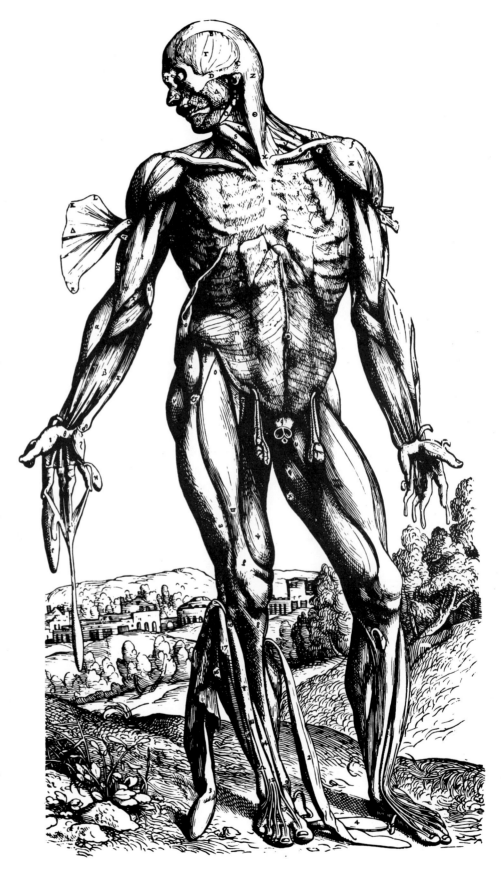

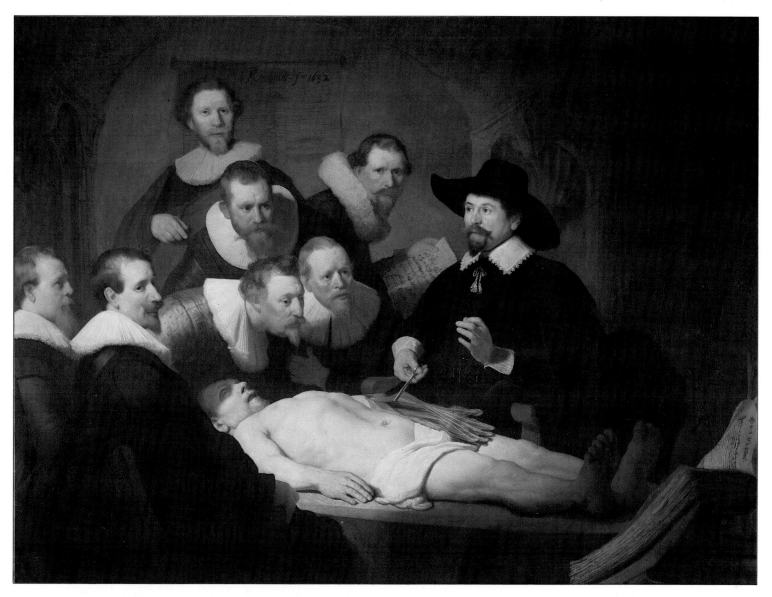

the only artist to conduct dissections; Albrecht Dürer (1471-1528), Donatello (c. 1386-1466), Michelangelo (1475-1564) and Raphael (1483-1520) are all known to have improved their knowledge of anatomy this way. There are also in existence a number of paintings of anatomy lessons which show the importance of the artist as a vehicle for social and scientific documentation, and the inherent interest of the subject.

The modern attitude to anatomizing is obviously more efficient than it was then, but even so, it is still unusual for art students to have access to real cadavers. However, thanks to the drawings of Leonardo and the many who followed in his footsteps, and more recently to excellent photographic reference, there need be no mystery for anyone who wishes to discover more about the workings of the human body.

The Principles of Anatomy

It is important for artists to be aware of the actual structure, or anatomy, of the body and to know how these various parts function together. The job of seeing and understanding what is happening to the outside of the body is greatly simplified if the artist realizes the causes of the various movements beneath the skin. Obviously, an artist's knowledge need not be as detailed as that of a doctor, who must understand the workings of the organs and the systems of the body in biochemical and biological terms. These need only concern the artist as far as they affect external appearances. However, to have a working knowledge of how the body fits together and to be able to recognize each part of the whole in any position and from any angle, greatly facilitates confident visual

Above *Anatomy Lesson of Doctor Nicolaes Tulp* (1632), Rembrandt. The Surgeons' Guild in Amsterdam commissioned Rembrandt to paint his first large group portrait, and the result guaranteed his position as Amsterdam's leading portrait painter for the next decade. In Holland there was an established tradition of official group portraiture and "anatomies" had already been painted by de Keyser (1596/7-1667) and others; however, these works were stiff and contained none of the emotional or pictorial strength visible in Rembrandt's pictures. By the middle of the seventeenth century, dissection had become an acceptable form of inquiry into the human condition, and anatomists important members of society.

suggested for the mixing and underpainting of skin color to allow just the right hue to shine through subsequent glazes. Before painting, variations in color and tone across the body must be carefully observed. Changes may occur depending on whether the bodily temperature or emotional mood of the model changes, or if he or she has recently been engaged in strenuous exercise.

An artist will often find that the surroundings also influence the color of flesh. Because of the reflective quality of skin, the nude figure picks up colors from objects around it which in turn greatly affect the mood of the painting. By surrounding the model with a deliberately chosen range of colors, the atmosphere can be altered and controlled. Painters sometimes compare colors which they are mixing with white, a piece of white paper for instance. This makes it easier to judge tone and make adjustments until the color is satisfactory.

An interesting example of the way in which color can be used in emotional terms to convey a particular mood is the painting of *The Dead Christ* by Hans Holbein (1497/8 – 1543). Holbein placed the figure against a background of cool greens and whites which are reflected in the face and hand. This contrasts with the treatment of the rest of the body, which in the shadows retains some of the warmer tones associated with living flesh. The stark and uncompromising pose and careful attention to anatomical detail combine with the deliberately simple and somber color to convey a horrifying image of death.

Victorious Amor, painted by the Italian Caravaggio (1573-1610) almost 100 years later, demonstrates an entirely different handling of the male nude. This figure is a lusty, golden boy whose glowing flesh reflects the warmth of the surroundings. The composition is more complex in both tonal and linear terms, although, like Holbein, Caravaggio chose to use a narrow color range to emphasize mood.

The use of drapery or clothing on the figure is, at its simplest, an extension of the skin and can be treated in a similar way. Just as with the nude there are certain bones and muscles which determine the surface form, so these continue to dominate the shape of the clothed body. Even when the figure is draped in an all-enveloping costume, the solidity of form can be retained by finding clues to the structure and concentrating on them more fully. Folds and creases often give an idea of the underlying structure. Drawing is a selective process; the trick is to know what to look for and to record those lines and masses which indicate the shape of the body while perhaps ignoring those which are merely transitory or superficial.

Manet's *Young Woman in an Oriental Costume*, painted toward the end of the nineteenth century, shows how, by adroit use of only a few simple folds, it is possible to imply the body underneath. The artist chose to paint this model in a costume which leaves only the head and forearms uncovered but is flimsy enough to allow tantalizing glimpses of the body beneath. The use of this sort of costume is a popular device because it allows the subject of the painting to retain a certain decency, while at the same time giving emphasis to the very parts which are concealed. A clothed or partly clothed figure may be more erotic than one which is totally nude, and especially so if the quality of the cloth itself is sensuous.

Just as the use of certain colors can evoke particular moods, so the choice of material clothing the figure can bring about differing emotional responses in the viewer. Some kinds of cloth are more clinging than others. The qualities of silk and satin are, for instance, not at all the same as those of wool or linen. The former are flimsy, lightweight materials which serve to cover the flesh while revealing the form, whereas the latter are thicker and retain much of their own character being less affected by the shape of the body underneath. The more tactile silks and satins are a popular choice when the female body is being represented as an object of desire.

The more robust types of cloth often reduce the figure to a simple outline which, depending on the purpose of the painting, can be satisfactory. Simplifying by a process of selection is common practice in all visual representation and made easier if the form is not complicated by elaborate, creasing clothes. Using large areas of flat color can give greater impact to other parts of the picture which are worked in more detail.

Where portraits have been commissioned the artist will often have been required to paint the sitter in some kind of formal dress, and this will necessarily have become an important element within the picture. Some of the most sumptuous and elegant portrait paintings show the subject displaying various signs of wealth and status. It is not surprising, after all, that the sitter should

Right *Girl with Shuttlecock,* Jean-Baptiste-Siméon Chardin (1699-1779). Chardin has provided much inspiration for many artists of the twentieth century in his natural handling of ordinary realistic forms. Apart from his stature as one of the greatest still-life artists, he is also famous for his treatment of modest, middle-class subjects. This reserved study of a young woman owes its charm to his skillful use of white, the simple formal drapery complementing the cool, settled pose.
Above right *Mealtime of the Officers of St Jorisdoelen,* Frans Hals. One of the great Dutch masters, Hals is primarily known as a portraitist. This group picture of civic guards is one of five he painted between 1620 and 1630, at the peak of his popularity. Hals is renowned for his ability to capture fleeting expressions; this group portrait suggests in its composition the ease and camaraderie of the guards. The drapery and clothing are an important part of this effect, the overall rhythm aided by the crisp angles of the starched ruffs, the texture and weight of the costly materials and the creases and directionals of the hanging cloth behind the figures.

Cloth studies
These details of cloth from Hals' *Mealtime of the Officers of St Jorisdoelen, Haarlem* illustrate the artist's mastery of paint. The rich heaviness of the furled silk banner, the almost transparent quality and delicacy of the two ruffs, their contrasting shapes emphasizing the artist's proficient handling of detail, the texture of the suede with its brilliant gold-embroidered decoration, and finally the luxurious sheen of the thick sash, are carefully evoked with tiny, almost invisible brush-strokes. The sense of realism and liveliness in the scene is enhanced by the volumes and textures of the various cloths.

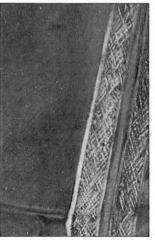

wish to be viewed by posterity looking at his or her best. In this type of work, the costume can dominate the painting, making a rich and intricate pattern of folds and pleats in a variety of textures and colors.

A typical example of highly elaborate costume is the portrait of Louis XIV by Rigaud (1649-1743), painted in 1701-2. The mood of artificiality in this painting is due partly to the obvious posing of the Sun King and partly to the overwhelmingly rich and heavy garments he is wearing. The painting is a flamboyant gesture, not only of the wealth and power of the subject of the painting, but also of the virtuosity of the artist. He shows his skill in representing fur, velvet and lace with great conviction and careful attention to minute detail. Although it was intended as a gift for his grandson, the King of Spain, Louis was so delighted with this image of himself that he decided to keep it.

Because of the constant changes in the world of fashion, paintings which portray clothes in the style of the time are important pieces of historical documentation. From this point of view, "genre" paintings, which show ordinary people doing everyday tasks, are even more valuable sources of information since they are not dependent upon the approval of the person paying. The artist has complete freedom to show reality even in its less attractive aspects. Hals (1581/5-1666), whose ability to produce elaborately detailed and highly finished paintings shows in such works as *Nurse and Child*, was probably at his best when producing genre paintings, when the freedom of his brushwork and masterly use of paint rival the Impressionists of two centuries later. In his painting *Malle Babbe*, Hals indicated the subject's clothing using broad strokes of color which suggest the form without describing it in detail. Her white cap and ruff are painted in high contrast to the dress which, like the rest of the painting, is dark and somber. This throws the head of the figure into sharp relief and gives emphasis to the almost maniacal expression on her face. The artist's use of white paint to pick out the highlights in energetic and jerky brushstrokes seems very much in keeping with this study of drunkenness and vulgarity.

It has been common practice for centuries to paint figures in contemporary costume in order to update old stories, so making them more relevant to the ordinary man or woman. Pre-Renaissance and Renaissance artists employed this device in their religious frescoes which helped to carry the message across to the illiterate faithful, showing characters from the Bible as ordinary people such as they might meet any day. This meant that the farmers, artisans and shopkeepers of the time could identify more easily with their

Biblical counterparts and recognize them as mortals rather than saints. It also meant that local dignitaries could increase their self-importance by modeling for the more illustrious characters represented.

Often, however, costume portrayed little contemporary or historical accuracy and was used simply as a means of giving structure and unity to a complicated composition. Mannerist painters from late sixteenth-century Italy, for instance, used swirls of drapery to give dramatic emphasis to the movement and gestures of their figures, filling the picture plane with activity. They included trailing swathes of cloth as an important element within the composition, rather than an accurate rendering of a garment which could actually be worn. These large and energetic paintings full of tumbling figures rely upon their curving masses of drapery to hold them together and, incidentally, to fill gaps which would otherwise reveal miles of landscape. The conviction with which the artists represented cloth hanging or billowing in the breeze is often countered by an air of unreality because of the bright, even brash,

Above *Giovanna Baccelli* (1782), Thomas Gainsborough (1727-88). In this full length portrait, the clothing is an important part of the composition, helping to convey a sense of movement and vitality. The pose, visible brushstrokes and blending of the figure into its landscape setting all increase the sensation of spontaneity and gaiety. In later life Gainsborough often painted his models using an unusual method — he placed his canvas the same distance away as his model, to form an angle of 90° between sitter, painter and canvas. Using a pair of fire tongs to hold his brush at arm's length he would then make marks on the canvas. The purpose of this technique was to lessen control over the brushmarks and to force himself to see the portrait in the same way as he saw the person posing in front of him. Gainsborough's understanding of character and anatomy was as profound as his love of landscape. It is interesting to note that, unlike other painters of the period, he painted all the drapery himself.
Right *The Clown Don Sebastian de Morra*, Velazquez. The unusual and direct pose of this dwarf, a jester from the Spanish court, reveals the strong human understanding and sympathy Velazquez brought to the art of portraiture. The warm background, lack of props and use of light and shade are all characteristic of his work.

colors and the overwhelming grandeur of the scenes.

To draw or paint the figure with conviction requires a sound working knowledge of its anatomy; similarly, the artist must investigate and become familiar with the anatomy of cloth to be able to make full use of the way its folds can emphasize or conceal. Artists' preliminary drawings often include careful studies of pieces of drapery. Numerous investigative sketches of this sort will encourage increasingly confident representations of a variety of textures and qualities. By noting how sharp creases give way to soft folds and by observing the differences between the character of free-hanging material and that which is draped over a solid object, the artist acquires a repertoire of visual language which can be used to inform paintings of the clothed figure.

An interesting experiment in drawing, and one that is frequently given to students in art schools, is to set up a still-life group using objects that have a clearly defined shape, such as boxes or bottles, and then to cover it with a plain piece of cloth. By softening the outlines the artist is forced to give greater consideration to tonal qualities and to treat the group of objects as a single, solid form in space. Individual details will be lost but a unity and monumentality will compensate. A very ordinary collection of objects can become mysterious and interesting when presented in this way. In the visual, as in other fields of art, the statement is often given greater potency by that which is left unstated.

Repeating this experiment but using, instead of the plain piece of cloth, a number of different, colored pieces, preferably with very positive surface patterning, will demonstrate how the entire effect can be changed although there is no alteration in the structure of the group itself. The character of the objects underneath will be dominated by the noisy chatter on the surface. By emphasizing the decorative quality of the cloth, the volume and solidity which were so positive in the previous group become far less apparent, and sometimes unrecognizable. It is easy, at this point, to move away from objective realism into the realms of abstract painting. Paint applied as flat areas of bright color will tend to destroy any illusion of depth. Using color and tone skillfully, an artist can control the level of abstraction. Many painters employ a system of simplifying and flattening shapes to arrive at pictures which, although figurative at the outset, no longer have any apparent link with the reality. Some find this a fascinating area for study and have devoted a great deal of time and energy expanding on this theme.

These same experiments can be tried using

Left *Mademoiselle Rivière* (1805), Jean Auguste Dominique Ingres. Typical of many portraits Ingres made of well-to-do sitters, this painting shows a sensitive treatment of the contours of the body, with the lines of the figure accentuated by the folds in the thin material of the dress. The angle of the elegant, long neck and uncovered chest, with the face turned towards the viewer, invites an inquisitiveness into the quality of her skin, the texture of which is made to contrast with the luxurious textures of the fur and satin. The curve of the fur reinforces the form of the face and shoulders, its delicate softness juxtaposed sensuously against the wrinkled gloves and the sheen of the satin ribbon.

people instead of objects underneath the drapes, and similar effects can be observed. A model posed in a reclining position will take on new dimensions when entirely covered by a large sheet. The interpretation of reality can become much more personal when the immediately recognizable aspects of the figure are hidden. Having learnt how to represent the figure as a working machine, the artist is free to focus attention on particular areas which can be distorted or disguised at will; the figure can be used as a starting point only, before moving on to highly subjective and fantastic images. The parallel between the draped figure and a gently rolling landscape has been exploited by a number of artists, some of whom have chosen to use this as a deliberate visual metaphor. When the viewer is forced to see the human figure from a new angle, its very familiarity makes it exciting.

Again, with a figure instead of a still-life, the disintegration of form which is caused by the imposition of a highly decorative covering can be used as an area for exploration and discovery. The ambiguity of solid form combined with flat pattern has stimulated the interest of many and prompted artists such as Pierre Bonnard (1867-1947), Paul Gauguin (1848-1903) and Henri Matisse (1869-1954) to make paintings which investigate the various possibilities. The strong influence of Orientalism which pervaded art of the nineteenth and early twentieth centuries is at its most apparent here. The emphasis is decorative and calligraphic and the figure becomes merely incidental. Gauguin considered a sense of mystery and decorative design to be two of the most important elements in art, and felt these aspects were being left behind by an age which was becoming increasingly mechanized and over-sophisticated. The scientific approach that had so excited the Impressionists had become, for Gauguin, a mere copying of nature, simple statements of fact which left little room for the imagination. He used the system of simplifying forms and colors until they made a decorative pattern in their own right and himself termed it "abstraction".

Gauguin's sojourn in the South Pacific was to have a profound effect on his work, bringing out essentially intuitive responses to what he saw. Guided by his respect for non-European art, he broke with the traditions laid down by the artists of the Renaissance and started the movement toward Expressionism and Surrealism. The paintings which he made during his time among the people of Tahiti, where he lived for some years between 1891 and his death, are concerned with creating a symbolic atmosphere without providing a logical explanation. He painted figures whose brightly patterned native dress argues with the exotic landscape in which they are set. The distinction between figures and background is minimal since Gauguin's love of strong colors and simple shapes makes for some paradoxical tonal and spatial relationships. His admiration of the savagery of primitive art forms combined with his passion for harmony and simplicity led him to make paintings which were lyrical and moody and yet hinted at religious and superstitious beliefs. His contemporaries found these results difficult to accept. During

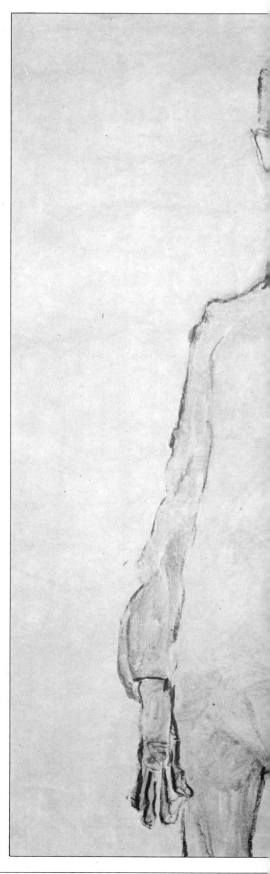

Right This cheerful study by Goya captures the subject arrested in the course of her movement. The treatment of costume here provides a vehicle for exploiting the contrast of light and dark, an interest Goya derived from his two greatest influences, Velazquez and Rembrandt. The straightened back and happy pose are emphasized by the hang of the clothes.
Center *Autoritratto* (1910), Egon Schiele (1890-1918). The artist was 20 when this drawing was made; only 28 when he died. At this point, his style is characterized by an Expressionist concern for emotional content. The clothing in this example is used to delineate the form beneath, the distortion and emaciation of the figure given added poignancy by the way the material gathers about the body.

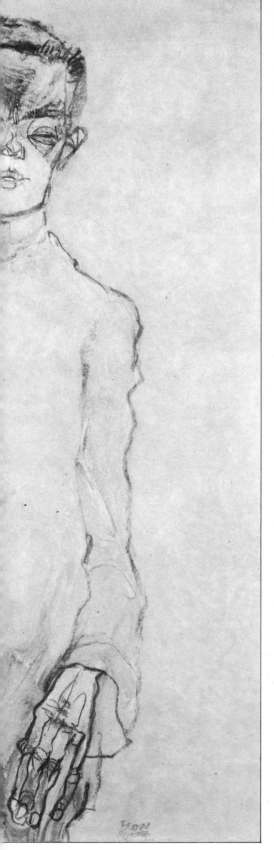

his lifetime he remained largely misunderstood and it was not until after his death that Gauguin's contribution came to be fully recognized and admired.

Gauguin died in 1903. His influence became apparent within a few years when a number of young French painters, including Matisse, Derain (1880-1954), Vlaminck (1876-1958) and Rouault (1871-1958), became known as the Fauves or "wild beasts" because of the intense savagery of their colors and images. In Germany, a group of Expressionist painters called *Die Brücke* aimed to create a new and anti-naturalistic form of painting. They represented the human figure in a deliberately brutal way using costume to slash in areas of color.

Matisse was the most important and influential painter among the Fauves and had a more deliberate and less spontaneous approach to painting than the Germans. Even so, his work, being fundamentally intuitive, fell within the Expressionist ideal. Like Gauguin, Matisse had a high regard for Oriental art and was concerned with the concept of simplicity. He painted his figures in simple lines and flat color, often using a single color, such as red or blue, to give the painting a great intensity of mood. He saw costume as a way of introducing ornamental pattern, although his aim was not simply to decorate but to express life itself.

In his later paintings he became almost obsessed by the nude figure although he retained the individual decorative quality of his paintings by setting them against brightly colored backgrounds. His *Pink Nude*, which was painted in 1935, moved close to total abstraction: the figure itself is a stylized outline, filled in with a hot pink with only arbitrary variations in hue. This is set against a large geometric area of brilliant blue and white checks, with further decorative elements being introduced by a strip of red and pink, a blob of bright yellow and more checks in green and white, all occupying the top third of the painting. Matisse said that his paintings used "beautiful blues, reds, yellows, matter to stir the sensual depths in men". He may be considered to have used the voluptuous color to symbolize the sexuality of his model.

Left *The Washerwoman* (1888), Henri de Toulouse-Lautrec. Around 1888, Lautrec became fascinated with portraying the ordinary people of the cafés, streets and theaters of Paris. The flat patterns and strong outlines of Japanese prints in this charcoal drawing of a washerwoman display another interest he developed at this time. The figure is treated almost as a silhouette, with the clothes serving to outline the overall shape and express character.

1. *Lorette VII (L'Echarpe Noire)*, Henri Matisse. The suggestive pose of this model is given added piquancy by the clinging, transparent material covering her body. Throughout his life, Matisse was particularly interested in the decorative aspects of pattern and color; in this painting the two strong patterns argue with each other, ironically allaying the interest in the nude figure glimpsed teasingly.

2. *Seated Woman in a Chemise* (1923), Pablo Picasso. The monumentality and calm grandeur of this figure almost gives it the appearance of classical sculpture. The angle of view helps to produce this effect as does the relative distortion of the hands and head. Another equally important element is the clothing; nominally a chemise, the thin drapery is arranged and depicted in such a way as to bring to mind the thin coverings of classical figures.

3. *Ea Haere Ia Oe* (1893), Paul Gaugin. Gaugin produced his finest work during his sojourns in the South Sea island of Tahiti. Here the costumes worn by the native women are derived from the real world, rather than the artist's imagination, the patterns on the material reflecting the natural surroundings, leaves, fruit and flowers. The painting gains its symbolic and emotional power through the tension which exists between the real activity portrayed by the artist and the action on the flat surface of the canvas — the way the colors, shapes and patterns work together.

2

3

4. *Quappi in Rosa* (1932), Max
Beckmann. This portrait
owes much of its power
to the full integration of tone,
color, composition and
brushwork. Although the
woman is in 1930s dress, this
does not detract from the strong
emotion or timeless quality of
the painting.

5. *The Travelling Companions*,
Augustus Egg (1816-1863). An
outstanding feature of this
painting is the delight with
which the artist has observed
the dresses. The composition
is a subtle play on a
mirror image, the eye being led
from figure to figure to spot the
small differences.

Matisse and those who followed him became increasingly excited by the abstract qualities in their work and for a time figurative art was not a popular element in modern painting. However, having taken abstraction to its logical conclusion, many artists have found it to be too limiting and have returned to figurative representations with a renewed interest.

How the artist chooses to dress a model today will be dictated to a large extent by the sort of painting he or she intends to produce. If it is with the human body itself that the artist is primarily concerned, then simple drapes will probably be preferred. This will allow a study of the way in which form is revealed by the rhythms of the cloth and the ways in which the figure exists as a solid object in space. To emphasize the bulk and volume of the figure, a single light source can be used which will reveal the model as a mass sculptured by light and tone.

It may be that the artist is interested by particular types of dress. Pablo Picasso (1881-1973) was fascinated by the theatricality of costume. He made paintings of Pierrots and Harlequins, often contrasting the gaiety of dress with the apparent melancholy of the model: the sad clown image. Edgar Degas (1834-1917) was another painter who was interested by theatrical dress. He made numerous studies of ballet dancers, which exploited his skill as a draftsman, and also visited the racetrack where he became engrossed in the particolored jockeys set against the green of the turf. Henri de Toulouse-Lautrec (1864-1901) frequented the circus where the combination of bright lights and garish costumes became a source for several of his paintings. Athletes, footballers, fighters and sportsmen are a favorite choice of subject matter, both

Right *Three Figures in an Attic.* In this modern oil painting of three figures in a garret room, the artist has created a still, cool atmosphere by establishing a single light source which bathes the models. Their stillness is further emphasized by the plain cut and somber colors of their clothing set against the steeply receding patterned carpet and bed, which isolate the figures from each other. The light-colored clothes of the man on the left emphasize his height, complementing the strong horizontals of the walls and door and the steeply angled diagonal over his head. A divorce is created between the standing figure and the two on the bed, not only through the positions and expressions on the faces but also through the contrast between the light- and dark-colored clothing, and the fact that the light falls most strongly on the standing figure.

Next, a smokey white glaze is worked over the floor and the figure given stronger white and yellow highlights. The focal point is shifted to the mirrored reflection, where a criss-cross pattern echoes the structure of the window frame (2). Another change of mind causes the form of the body to be reinforced with some darker greens and browns. Masking tape prepares for precise lines to be added to the window frame, and the towel gains highlights (3). Finally, brighter lights are added to the figure and the haziness is recreated with another thin, white-blue glaze.

The woman's fingers catch direct sunlight, and the towel becomes flatter in tone with decorative red stripes. The most important change, however, is in the basic construction of the picture. Right at the end, the ceiling is heightened and the top of the window straightened to increase the spaciousness of the room (4).

4

Above *Man and Woman in a Garden*. In this modern oil painting, the man's figure emerges from the shadows into the light, the sense of movement created by the broken outlines of the body as it is obscured by the green of the tree, and contrasting with the absolute stillness of the woman sitting in the full glare of the sunlight.

Left *Runners on the Beach (No 2).* The movement of these cardboard cut-out figures, deliberately depicted in a naive, semi-geometric style, is achieved by the several figures, all in obvious running positions, being crowded together, and by the juxtaposition of the colors.

Far left These three thirty-second pencil sketches of a girl taking off her stockings demonstrate how a few simple lines can give the impression of movement. Short poses are good practice, teaching the artist the ability to react quickly to small movements and forcing the description of instantaneous impressions while walking around the figure.
Left These rapid sketches show how the artist has captured the essence of the movement of the figure in simple lines.
Above *Girl Lying in a Window.* The artist has brilliantly captured the sense of the model rolling over, ecstatically kicking up her legs. The figure is placed within the yellow embrasure of a window, its darkish form outlined against the window and the gold of the cornfield, with the light falling on its contours. This painting, the result of much overpainting as the model's position changed, demonstrates the liveliness of the oil medium.

NUDE BY BALCONY
oil on hardboard 3 × 4½ feet (91 × 137 cm)

A board or wood support is solid enough to take a hard gesso primer without fear of the primer cracking as it would on canvas. The gesso ground, a mixture of whiting and size, is applied thickly in four layers, each layer being rubbed smooth before the next is added. Beneath this, rabbit skin glue size is applied in two coats and left to dry. In this particular work, the first laying in of color was in oil paint, diluted with genuine spirit of turpentine. When dry, the surface was developed by overpainting, with a little more linseed oil added to the turpentine at each stage. The artist took care to leave certain designated areas, parts of the floor for example, completely white. The process of building up the color and elaborating and enriching using increasingly thick paint on subsequent layers, can be taken further by using stand oil instead of linseed in the later stages. If it is felt that some parts of a work are inconsistent with others because the color seems to be "sinking in", then retouching varnish applied with an atomizer will bring any color back to its true liveliness. This very diluted varnish can also be obtained in aerosol spray cans. It does not leave a harsh, shining surface to make overpainting difficult and is a useful aid when a picture has been left between stages for some time. This picture took some extensive compositional changes, making overpainting essential.

The initial oil painting is made with a limited range of colors. Cobalt blue and Payne's grey are used for the background, while shades of green and yellow are used for the figure and the main areas of shadow. A large proportion of the painting is left white to suggest the strong sunlight streaming through the open door. All the main shapes and relationships are established at this stage, but there is considerable scope for change (1).
Details are built up in all the background areas of the painting. A lace curtain is added at the window to the left of the picture; the artist is here experimenting with ways of balancing the strong diagonal created by the left arm as it slopes down to the floor. A vivid pattern is overpainted on the bed and a large pillow added behind the figure's head, easing the conjunction with the wall. These decorative details serve to create a surface interest on the blocks of color (2).

1

4

2

More detail is built up in the background of the picture. Strong vertical lines indicate the balcony railings; these are painted with the use of masking tape to ensure straight edges. Curtains elaborate the door frame and the lace curtain is extended up into the window area. The areas of white in the painting are almost entirely constituted of untouched, gesso-primed board; they maintain the high contrasts (3). The next stage of the painting begins to show evidence of a change in the artist's basic intentions. The red and yellow added to the highlight area on the left leg and arm suggest a later time of day in that the

intensity of the light has modified. The introduction of these colors alters the overall mood of the painting, softening it. The artist decides to remove the lace curtain and strengthen the window area to match the severity of the door frame. A hint of green in the view from the door suggests that further interest will develop here. The figure, too, is in the process of readjustment, with an attempt being made to interrelate arms and legs more closely. Such changes have a surprisingly dramatic effect on the overall atmosphere of the painting. Although the basic shapes have remained constant, additions to the color range have altered

our perception of the monumental form of the figure and the shape of the highlights and shadows. The decorative details have also added a new dimension. One great advantage of painting in oils is that it allows for such major changes in emphasis; considerable experiment can be accommodated within one painting (4).

FIGURE IN CONTEXT

The context of a painting is, in a pure sense, any suggestion of a background or setting which locates the figure in space. It is possible to represent the figure without indicating surroundings, but when it comes to finished works, particularly paintings, artists are inevitably involved with some notion of context. The background may be abstract, even of a totally plain color; more usually, the artist places the figure in a setting which gives an idea, sometimes very precise, of the world the figure inhabits. The details of the setting may also imply the world the artist inhabits, as they often provide essential clues to man's self-image at any one time, revealing certain moral and ideological preoccupations. In this country, in an age of relatively free expression, they tend to reveal the artist's personal viewpoint.

Artists have not always had the freedom to present the figure in any chosen manner, as is generally considered possible now. Social and moral constraints have at times proved too powerful to be ignored, and have often prevented artists from being honest or explicit. The artist of the Middle Ages was little more than the humble bearer of God's word. Since then, classical notions of beauty and the purity of the human form, derived from Greek representations of the body, have provided both an enduring artistic ideal and a convenient excuse for portraying the naked form during periods when such exposure was frowned upon. In the same way, religious, mythological or historical themes could be called upon to furnish safe backdrops for artists to display their primary interest.

In the Renaissance, the beauty of the human figure was openly appreciated as it had been in Greek and Roman times, although it was still felt that the themes of paintings, whether they included nude figures or not, had to be based in either myth or religion. Carrying this tradition into the nineteenth century, Jacques-Louis David (1748-1825) painted the nude figure with the notion that it was justifiable if the figure "represented the customs of antiquity with such an exactitude that the Greeks and Romans, had they seen the work, would not have found me a stranger to their customs". Under the patronage of Napoleon, the politically motivated work of this artist came to be highly influential, reflecting the new cult of devotion to duty and austerity in France at the time.

Another French painter in this classical mold was Ingres (1780-1867), who studied in David's studio. Despite the apparently detached quality of his work, he was an emotional and imaginative artist and came to be accepted as the champion of a classical idealism, completing works with titles such as *The Triumph of Romulus over Acron* (1812) and *Apotheosis of Napoleon* (1853).

Two centuries earlier, in mid-seventeenth-century Spain, the great Velazquez painted his only nude, the *Rokeby Venus*. Spain was particularly slow in relaxing the strict moral code of the Middle Ages, and the work must have been considered severely shocking. In spite of its classical disguise which led Velazquez to add, as an apparent after-thought, a cupid holding up a mirror into which the reclining nude is looking, there is a freshness and lack of idealization in the painting. This is partly due to the unusual pose, with the figure seen from behind, which allowed her a freedom from coyness because the viewer is unapprehended. Mirrors are often considered useful props; they allow the viewer to glimpse the subject from another angle, so reinforcing the three-dimensional sense of space.

By contrast, in the mid-eighteenth-century French court of Louis XV, blatantly erotic nudity was accepted and encouraged. Works by François Boucher and Jean Fragonard for example, show little attempt to render the indecent decent in mythological disguise; even the pretence of classical respectability was abandoned. These paintings reflect the taste for frivolity and exaggerated gallantry prevalent in the French court at that time.

In northern Europe the desire to be rid of pretence and disguise manifested itself in a different way, and led to a fashion in genre painting exemplified by such Dutch works as *Boy Removing Fleas from his Dog* by Ter Borch (1617-81) and *A Woman and her Maid in a Courtyard* by de Hooch (1629-83). The paintings of Jan Vermeer of Delft (1632-75) are in a similar style although they demonstrate his particular mastery of color and the effects of light falling into a room. He often chose everyday, domestic scenes for subject matter, such as *Maid Servant Pouring Milk* or *Music Lesson*.

Left *Job Mocked by his Wife*, Georges de la Tour. The subject of this painting is not the figures, which would have little interest taken separately out of context, but the emotion expressed between them. This is emphasized by the single candle, its light creating a world for them and cutting out the background. Sympathy for Job's vulnerability is evoked by his wife's overbearing attitude and the gesture of her hand as well as his nakedness and low position. The simplified forms of this painting give it a deceptively modern appearance; in fact, they are often considered to reflect a revival of interest in the Franciscan way of life which took place in Lorraine, where de la Tour worked, in the early seventeenth century.

Above *The Lacemaker*, Jan Vermeer of Delft. The context of this genre painting is domestic, and the scene is informal and unpretentious, with the lacemaker's accoutrements scattered in seemingly haphazard disarray. The composition is, however, beautifully designed: the strong lines of her hair, collar and arms, of the cushion and the edge of her worktable are all directed towards her hands, to the action she is making, so allowing the viewer to share her concentration, as if sitting just in front of her. The portrait is charming and intimate because the subject and the setting are natural; it is a simple comment on the everyday life of a young girl.

A similar authenticism was propounded by the self-named Pre-Raphaelite Brotherhood painters in Victorian England. The founder members of this group, Dante Gabriel Rossetti (1828-82), Holman Hunt (1827-1910) and John Everett Millais (1829-96), stated their aim as a desire to return to a more natural life than the new enthusiasm for machinery allowed; their inspiration was the world of medieval romance. In their determination to present verity they worked a great deal from life and included careful detail in their paintings. Hunt, in particular, produced work of great seriousness and historical accuracy, even traveling to Palestine in order to give his pictures an authentic flavor.

Working at the same time in France was Gustave Courbet. He began painting in the age-old classical tradition that, in the shadow of David and Ingres, was still prevalent in early nineteenth-century France, but soon began to develop the individual style that was to cause an uproar among contemporary art critics. The classical tradition had grown stale, and much painting could be classified as either pedantically academic or sweetly sentimental; in reaction to this, Courbet set himself up as the leader of the Realist school of painting. He chose subjects from contemporary life, not excluding what was usually considered ugly or vulgar. He deliberately rejected the intellectual and premeditated approach to painting, preferring instead to react instinctively to the power of nature. He made numerous paintings on the themes of woman as an organic earth-mother figure, of the sea and of the fruitfulness of nature shown best by mighty trees at harvest time. He was a great believer in the joy and glory of life. However, by highlighting the plight of the ordinary working man and giving significance to mundane activities, Courbet was as good as asking for the inevitable abuse which continued unabated through much of his life.

Another painter whose work could be classed as Realism in a similar vein was Honoré Daumier (1810-79), although he was more politically motivated than Courbet. He used his paintings and caricatures to bring the plight of the poor into public consciousness, vesting the humblest of themes and the meanest of situations with weight and dignity.

The nineteenth century was a time of upheaval in Europe, mostly due to social and economic changes. Reflecting the turbulence, some artists assumed a similar role to that of modern photojournalists, deeming that art should mirror all aspects of life. Goya (1746-1828), a Spanish painter, produced the dramatic *Shooting of the Rebels on May Third*

Above *Mr and Mrs Andrews,* Thomas Gainsborough. This painting of local gentry in a landscape setting has an elegant and carefree atmosphere. The richness of the countryside and the play of light over the grass enhance the context, and perfectly match the mood of the couple. Gainsborough's style was well suited to the pastoral fashions and tastes of the eighteenth century, and his artistry was much in demand.

Left *Linda Maestra,* Goya. The eerie, night setting of this bizarre etching provides an evocative background for an unusual subject. The coarse wispiness produced by the etching technique reinforces the texture of the witches' hair and the twigs in the broomstick. Despite a lack of detail, the weird and macabre impression is powerful.

Right *The Awakening Conscience* (1853), Holman Hunt. The Victorian setting of this picture is rich and colorful, full of strong, mixed patterns and ornate detail. Hunt's portrayal may be viewed as a realistic representation of a middle-class interior; however, the lavish detail may also be seen to make a mockery of the girl's position as the man's mistress, over-emphasizing her material gain at the moment that she realizes her folly. There is a strong moral emphasis in this Pre-Raphaelite painting.

representing scenes of everyday life in cafés, restaurants, on the street, by rivers, in bedrooms, bathrooms, and dining rooms, and recent developments in photography led them to compose their pictures in a spontaneous and inconsequential manner reminiscent of the snapshot. Figures were often presented half out of the picture. But more important than the content was their technique. It had become known that all color and form is perceived as a series of patterns on the retina, and the eye does its own color mixing. Their aim was to recreate the brilliance of sunlight and the effects of light on local color. The intensity of their color harmonies was due to the use of complementary colors in the shadows. If the light part of an object was green, for instance, then the darker areas would display red. They expelled black from their palettes.

The direct and painterly way in which the Impressionists expressed their ideas and the vitality and freshness of their work created a new mood in painting. They were concerned with "truth", but they shifted the emphasis away from content. They wanted to take no moral or religious stand; it was therefore important to paint people or things where no meaning other than the purely visual impact was implied.

Because the eye can only focus on a relatively small area at one time, these painters were obliged to dispense with fine detailing in order to convey the general impression. Some of the Impressionists, Monet in particular, became so involved in the pursuit of the ephemeral effects of light that solid form became dissolved in the total atmosphere of his paintings.

Often the Impressionists' paintings of the nude figure are sensual but unerotic. This is largely because the quality of sensuality is as much to do with the handling of the paint and the artist's obvious joy in the effects of light as it is to do with the represented nature of the model. Even so, the sunlight dappling across female flesh in some of Renoir's paintings, and the delicate backlighting behind the nudes by Bonnard provide effects that are more tactile than intellectual.

Seurat (1859-91) took the Impressionist ideas to their logical extension – Pointillism. In some of his paintings, including *The Bathers*, he totally abandoned the use of colors mixed on the palette, covering his canvas instead with tiny dots of primary color in varying combinations, leaving the eye of the viewer to mix them optically. He was also aware of the phenomenon of "irradiation", of any color in nature being surrounded by its complementary color, and used this theory in his pictures.

Seurat's "divisionist" technique involved calculating the quantities of various colors

1808 inspired by his resistance to French military rule which existed under Joseph Bonaparte between 1808 and 1814, and also produced 65 brutally savage etchings entitled *The Disasters of War.* David, who was in active sympathy with the French Revolution, painted three portraits of the martyrs of the Revolution – Marat, Lepeletier and Bara. These and other paintings are visual documentation of political events. Goya and David took Realism to an extreme, intending to record and shock.

With Courbet painting scenes from everyday life, and great scientific progress being made through the nineteenth century, the path was paved for the Impressionist painters, such as Monet (1840-1926), Renoir, Manet and Pissarro (1830-1903). Their struggle against classicism is evident in Renoir's *Diana* and Manet's *Olympia;* however, the most important aspect of their painting was their use of light and color, This was a revolutionary, scientific approach to painting. They became famous for

Right *The Bathers*, Georges Seurat. Partly as a result of reading Chevreul's book on colour theory (first published 1839) and Charles Henry's observations on the aesthetics of light, Seurat evolved his "divisionist" technique. He built up the figures in his paintings with a great number of dots or strokes of local color combined with the colors from the sky and surrounding objects; in shadows he included the complementary colors of proximate areas of light.

Far right An illustration for *The Rape of the Lock*, Aubrey Beardsley. Recognizably in Beardsley's linear style, this black and white drawing displays some exemplary eighteenth-century details, such as the decorations on the table and the style of the wall moldings, to place the figure in the context of the poem by Alexander Pope. The almost abstracted area of the gown, stippled with a floral pattern, makes a strong, flat contrast against the blocked-in floor.

Below right *The Restaurant Entrance*, Jean Louis Forain. Much in the style of Honoré Daumier, Forain delighted in making satirical comments on society in his paintings and drawings. Strong emotions are expressed in a few simple lines and washes in this watercolor painting.

present and placing them as separate dots on the canvas. The picture so produced had then to be viewed from the correct distance, when the dots would appear to mix and blend, achieving greater luminosity than would be possible had the colors been mixed on the palette.

Although Impressionism began as a lively and forward-looking movement, it quickly staled. The artists involved had so whittled down scientific naturalism to a purely optical matter that there was no further progress to be made. By the end of the nineteenth century, influenced by the real threat of the camera, there was a strong reaction against the idea that the artist is a copier of nature, and instead there was a feeling that the artist should use paint as a means of self-expression.

The paintings of Vincent van Gogh were dedicated to making people think and to

bring them to understand the comfort and warmth of love. He wanted to express through his paintings the universal power of light. He learnt from the Old Masters and from the Impressionists but eventually developed his own style, working from the observation of real things and real people, in a highly subjective manner. He simplified form and exaggerated the drawing and the color. His real sympathy for the peasants who had to scratch a living from the land is apparent in the way he emphasized the squareness and solidity of a workman in order to give expression to the idea of hard labor. The warmth of his emotions and his reaction to the wonders of nature are expressed by his vibrant use of orange to represent sunlight. Like the Impressionists, he was fond of using complementary colors and found that he could set one off against the other to further intensify the emotional

content. By working in this purely subjective way, he found that his use of drawing and color was becoming more symbolic and that this in turn was leading to a flattening of the picture plane.

Van Gogh's treatment of the human figure was one of sympathy and passion. His own anguish and suffering which led to his eventual suicide were expressed in his paintings as a feeling of isolation. He often painted single, stolid figures which seemed to suggest that they were more at home with the soil than with one another. The autobiographical element is strong in his paintings. He felt that what he had to say would only have significance if it was born of his own experience. It was this which led him to abandon ambitious themes such as *Christ's Agony in the Garden* and replace them with more personally relevant ones. His emphasis on personal feeling marked him out as one of

the forerunners of Expressionism.

Gauguin, also working expressively, did not use color as a purely visual record of the effects of light. He was more interested in the way that color can be used to evoke mood and emotion. Working with large areas of flat, unbroken color, his pictures became mysterious and decorative designs. His paintings of the figure demonstrate an authority in drawing which was subjugated by his feeling for pattern and color. The inherent savagery which is present in all his paintings, particularly his self-portraits, prepared the way for the Fauves.

However, the most influential Post-Impressionist was Paul Cézanne (1839-1906), who believed that personality could only be developed to the full when in close contact with nature. Although Cézanne is remembered for his sensitive treatment of landscape, in his early years as a painter he

was indifferent to this subject, and produced large figurative works. Throughout his life he was obsessed by the theme of bathers. His early studies, which he made directly from the model, were coarse and frequently erotic. He attacked the canvas with great ferocity, laying on the paint in thick slashes with a palette knife. His unconventional approach to drawing prevented him from ever fulfilling his ambition to paint more academic nudes after the fashion of Delacroix. In his old age he painted distorted and stylized figures from photographs or from the imagination. His simplifications of the female nude, which often seem less than human, nevertheless conform to classical compositional devices. His large painting *The Bathers*, which he was working on in the years leading up to his death, has a triangular composition into which are fitted apparently clumsy and shapeless female figures. Cézanne defined form and structure by an infinite variation of tone, and space by the use of well regulated receding planes. If the underlying geometric structure sometimes makes his work appear severe, then the subtle variation of line and tone lend it a lyricism which has been admired and emulated ever since.

The Fauves, a group of French painters working at the beginning of the twentieth century, were so called because their treatment of day-to-day scenes was considered wild and animalistic. In their use of rhythmic line the influence of Cézanne can be discerned, but their use of bright color and pattern was more cheerful and decorative. Their paintings of the figure were energetic and uninhibited. The aim was to produce compositions which were expressive as a whole without relying on details.

At the same time Georges Rouault was painting more violently Expressionist pictures than other French artists. He was a religious artist who is best known for the stained-glass effect of his paintings with bright colors outlined heavily in black. Between 1904 and 1910 he painted brutal pictures of prostitutes, corrupt judges and so on, using sour, dirty colors and shockingly incorrect drawing.

The development of graphic art has greatly influenced painting in this century. At the end of the nineteenth century, there was less of a distinction between "fine art" and "graphic art". Many important artists of this time were not only painters but also poster designers. The flat pattern quality which had been such a feature of the work of Gauguin and was being exploited so well by Matisse, Kandinsky (1866-1944) and Rouault, was particularly suitable for printed designs. Printing techniques, in turn, played an important part in the final decision to reject perspective in favor of surface shapes; this

Above *Mr and Mrs Clark and Percy* (1970), David Hockney. All the objects depicted in this scene are naturalistically represented to give a subtle impression of their volumes and their positions in space. There is a fine, lyrical quality to the white lilies. However, the lack of surface detail seems to imply that Hockney deliberately abstracted the forms, choosing certain features specifically and leaving others out; also that the objects themselves were deliberately chosen. The result is an inconsistent view of reality, an example of the artist's Expressionist style of painting. The Clarks were painted in their home, in a sunny and relaxed setting, with the viewer in the position of a guest.

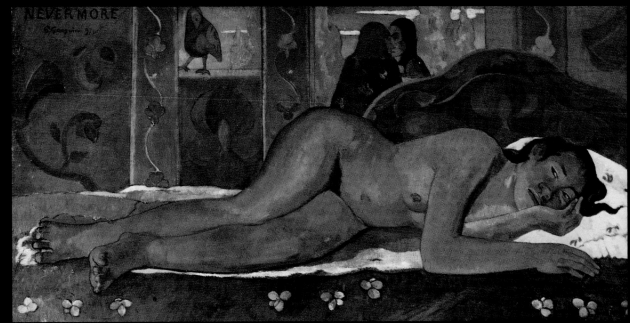

Far left *Nevermore*, Paul
Gauguin. With great sympathy
for the subject, Gauguin painted
this intimate portrait of a young
girl asleep. All the paintings of
his later life have an extreme
individuality of style, partly
because the subjects and
landscapes are those of the
South Sea islands where he
lived, which, being so different
from his native France, greatly
influenced him. He painted the
people and the landscapes not
just for the sake of recording
them, however, but also to
record his reactions to the
primitive lifestyle. He was
sensitive to the tropical colors
and unusual patterns and forms
and incorporated them to create
powerful images of natural
innocence and simplicity.
Left *Harlem* (1934), Edward
Burra (1905-1976). The city
context of this watercolor
painting was inspired by a visit
that Burra made to New York in
1934. The vivid impression of
the lifestyle of the native New
Yorkers is conjured up by the
brittleness of the medium and
the juxtaposition of harsh and
soft textures. The brick, tarmac,
paving and iron contrast with the
clothes, the blue jacket, pink
shirt and green Homburg hat,
and also with the fur. Simplified
forms and a peculiar perspective
which almost implies that the
upper windows are stuck to the
wall instead of being a part of it,
are all part of the disjointed
atmosphere.

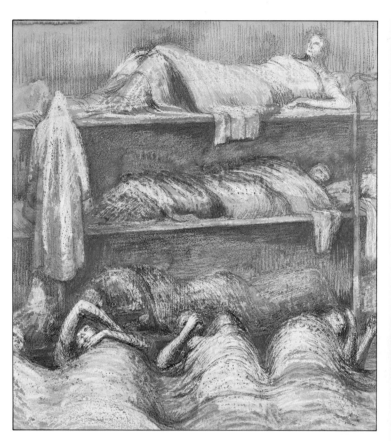

Right *Shelter Scene,* Henry Moore (b. 1898). The dreariness of waiting out the air-raids in shelters and underground stations during the Second World War is emphasized by the somber coloring of this drawing. drawing. Despite the monumentality with which Moore characteristically imbues his figures, the setting is crowded and a feeling of claustrophobia is implied by the heavy, overlaid lines.
Far right *The Call of Night,* Paul Delvaux (b. 1897). The dreamlike quality of this painting by the Belgian artist who was influenced by de Chirico and Magritte, is typically Surrealist in style. The references within the picture, despite being meticulously painted, are denied any consistency and therefore coherence. The picture describes a totally unrealistic and contrary scene, for example, the trees are bare while the nudes are growing long bushes of leaves from their heads. The viewer is mystified and prompted to question reasons for the existence of the objects and the relationships between them.

led inevitably toward total abstraction of form. Artists such as Henri de Toulouse-Lautrec and Aubrey Beardsley (1872-98) were primarily interested in the figure but represented it in a way which was already halfway toward the abstract. Beardsley's black and white drawings use elongated and attenuated forms and contrast large and simple shapes with areas of fine detail. Toulouse-Lautrec dispensed with modeling in depth in favor of emphasizing the surface plane. His use of the calligraphic line and bright splashes of color produced images which are both decorative and sensitive descriptions of the human figure.

As artists experimented with new and exciting media the distinction between painting and sculpture became less obvious. Cubism, developed at the beginning of the century by Pablo Picasso and Georges Braque (1882-1963), became, in its final stage, a mixture of drawing, painting and collage. The Cubist method of treating the composition as an arrangement of geometrically shaped planes related to the rectangular plane of the picture was a clear influence on abstract art, but however abstracted their work became during certain periods, Picasso and Braque never lost interest in the human figure as a source of inspiration.

Picasso treated the backgrounds of his Cubist paintings in the same way as the figures. The form is fragmented and so is the space, making it difficult to translate. But Picasso does provide visual clues which help the viewer to recognize his familiar environment in the painting. In *Les Demoiselles d'Avignon* the figures are surrounded by what, at first, seem to be incomprehensible shapes. Then at the bottom of the canvas is a small still-life of fruit: a melon, pears and grapes. Suddenly the figures seem to be enclosed by folds of drapery, which are perhaps curtains. The eye and brain demand meaning from the visual work and where something is not fully explained, the imagination takes over.

The abstraction of some of Henri Matisse's paintings often does little more than give an implication of surroundings. In *The Dance,* for instance, there is no more than a simple division of the canvas into two shapes. In the lower half is a mound-like form which can be seen as a grassy hillock, although the only real basis for presuming as much is that it is colored green. Similarly, the rest of the canvas is a deep and intense blue, which may be the sky. The conventions of childhood insist that grass is green and sky is blue and the instinctive reaction to these colors being used in conjunction with the figure is to interpret them accordingly.

Some painters choose to keep the background simple but to include certain selected items almost in the way that a stage director uses props to set the scene for a play. Otto Dix (1891-1969), whose work is particularly interesting because he used mixed media including egg tempera, employed this contextual device. He painted figures against a background flooded with almost flat color, and then included a small number of pertinent details: a carefully painted marble table top, a cocktail glass, a box of matches, a packet of cigarettes. All the details are rendered with precision and are

Above *Dammerung 22,* George Grosz. Strong reactions to Germany's social corruption prompted Grosz to draw brutal caricatures; society reacted by persecuting him with some frequency for insulting public morals. This watercolored drawing ironically juxtaposes two people of questionable character conversing in the foreground with a veteran who is forced to sell matches for a living.

chosen because they are immediately evocative of a particular atmosphere.

Cézanne and Matisse were both fascinated by bathing figures, and the backgrounds they included often gave only minimal information. An indication of a tree or a suggestion of figures dressing or undressing are sufficient to suggest the subject matter. David Hockney (b. 1937) has continued this technique using Beverley Hills swimming pools as the background for a number of his paintings. Again, there is not a great deal of visual information. He fills his canvas with large areas of blue and white, finding hard-edged shapes in the ripples and splashes of water.

Surrealist painters, by contrast, used deliberately complex backgrounds to suggest eerie and mysterious atmospheres with no firm and comprehensible linking references. De Chirico (1888-1978) produced strange effects using strong tonal contrasts and several eye-levels. *Secret and Melancholy of a Street* shows a solitary girl playing in an empty street, but at the far end an unseen figure casts a long shadow across her path. Painters such as Magritte (1898-1967) placed their figures in incongruous situations to create similar feelings of discomfort.

Artists reflect their personal vision in paintings, but also the age in which they live. Some artists are aware of the need to place figures against a truly contemporary background. This idea directly opposes the idea behind abstract paintings which contain no particular reference, so implying a universal context. The problem of creating contemporary settings is much greater now than ever before, as objects and styles become dated and tend to look old-fashioned increasingly quickly against the pace of progress. By including a symbol of the modern age such as a television, which was used by Richard Hamilton (b. 1922), a modern atmosphere can be conveyed. However, changing styles of interior decoration make it easy to date a television from the 1960s, and a painting becomes emphatically out-of-date because of the very technique used to create the opposite effect.

One solution to this problem, which might be considered a gimmick, was found by the artist Michelangelo Pistoletto (b. 1933), whose pictures of life-size figures are painted onto a mirrored surface which reflects the surrounding space. In this way, the figures are always in a contemporary context.

SEATED NUDE BY WINDOW
pastel and chalk on paper 20 × 15 inches (51 × 38 cm)

Pastel is a delicate medium, providing a range of brilliant colors and the possibility of working one over others until the result almost looks white. Chalks are more incisive, harder and produce fine lines, allowing the artist to draw with a vigor impossible in pastel. Both these media allow the artist to work light over dark and make changes or adjustments while work is in progress. Models are likely to move, however subconsciously or surreptitiously, while they are posing, and in order to keep the picture alive, the artist must be able to respond to these changes. Often, a particular pose will not suit a model and he or she will move to a more natural, comfortable position. This encourages the creation of more natural and lively drawing. Such changes need not totally obliterate the original work.

1

2

The model's first pose, with both feet touching the floor and her head twisted to look out of the window, proves uncomfortable, and despite the initial drawing already being established, the model moves to a position in which she can relax. The two strong lines of her back and her left leg need only slight readjustment and the positions of her neck, head, arms and right leg are changed, although the points of reference remain constant. The first sketches are made in blue pastel, the artist feeling for the pose and quickly relating angles and positions (1, 2). With some solid work in shades of blue and red, areas of the figure are shaded and the form fills out.

3

4

6

The whole picture is worked using a complex system of laying and overlaying colors in different combinations, so that the underlayers show through. The result is an overall sense of unity and a subtle feeling for form. Positive background shapes are laid in blocks of color (3).

The patterns of the background cloth are ignored, and a single color is implied, with brighter pastels used nearer the light source. Using the heavier

chalks, earth reds and browns are added to bring out the form of the figure, and build up the arm of the chair over the background blue (4).
Chalks and pastels combine for the bold stripes of the carpet, which provide a tension with the diagonal of the chair. White and yellow highlights in both pastel and chalk, which is illustrated in this close-up (5), give a strong impression of the indirect sunlight falling into the room. Some of these are blended and

smudged into the colors beneath, with further lights added in the final stage. Hatching with contrasting pastels over the already blended and fixed colors creates final subtle shading. Indigos and blues are used over the left thigh, and pinks over the chest and left arm (6).

5

NUDE ON GREEN BED
oil on canvas 3 × 4½ feet (91 × 137 cm)

2

3

A small watercolour sketch (1) acts as a reminder of the composition. Using thin, summarizing tones of indigo and white, the first layers are laid and strong horizontals established against the bright, abstracted patches of sunlight (2). More intense pinks and yellows are worked over the shapes of the figure and the bed, giving localized impressions of volume and decoration (3). The lines of the bed are made to conform to the edges of the painting and pattern is brought to the right side of the canvas (4). It is an endlessly adjusting basis for further elaboration.

4

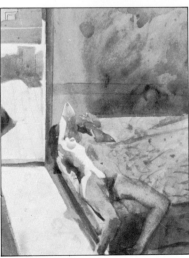

1

Making a sketch in watercolor to record information about a situation is an efficient way of preparing for an oil painting, particularly if the subject or the light is transitory. It also helps the artist to establish tonal values spontaneously and decisively as watercolor is a more demanding medium in this respect, changes being difficult to make after a wash has been laid.

Later, using oils on a fine, well-primed canvas, the artist decided to change the composition of the painting from the vertical proportions of the original watercolor to the horizontal, while also reducing the size of the figure in relation to the size of the support. By using a long horizontal, a feeling of calm relaxation is gained, reflecting the pose of the nude girl, and the composition balanced by the addition of a light-source on the right. Basic decisions regarding shape and size of supports should not be lightly dismissed, as emotional reactions to different proportions vary. The shape of a tall, gothic spire, for example, often suggests an urgency and symbolizes high ideals or aspirations. The square, the circle and rectangles of all proportions carry inescapable emotional associations, often dependent on individual experiences. Similarly, particular compositional rhythms are better suited to particular overall shapes. A simple rectangle to the proportions of one to two, or two to three, suits strongly structured surface patterns using diagonals. Such compositions bring with them noise and energy, which is in marked contrast to the calm and quietude employed in this work. The mood is enhanced by the use of a limited palette.

GIRL BY WINDOW WITH BLINDS
watercolour and gouache on paper 18 × 28 inches (46 × 71 cm)

This is an example of watercolor being used, mostly in its pure form, to describe the effects of light in a bright and airy room. The white of the paper shines through the thin washes giving the painting a luminosity which also existed in reality.

Attention is divided between the window and the figure, both potentially being the subject. Light-sources are often more difficult to control inside the picture than outside when the effects of light can be exploited without including a dominating rectangle of light. However, including a window or open door presents a large number of challenging compositional structures and effects.

Here, the artist holds the shape of the window by enclosing it in darker tones, the window itself being mainly represented by the untouched white of the support. The strength of this image and the shimmery effect of the blinds provide a strong basis, allowing the painter to present a sympathetic interpretation of the seated girl in the interior.

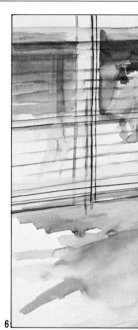

The pose is arranged to obtain a quick study of light quality. The upper part of the model, leaning against a cushion, is silhouetted against a white wall. The hard lines of the Venetian blind form diagonals and contrast with the softer shapes of the bed and the figure of the model (1). The first ideas of the composition are mapped out lightly in watercolor on fine-grained Ingres paper stretched out on a board with a gum strip (2).

The green sap of the trees is painted over the broken brown lines which show through the watery green wash, emphasizing the dissolution of forms in light (3).

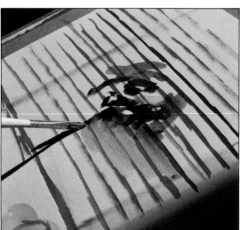

The two basic themes, the shimmering effect of light on the trees through the blinds and the light on the bed and the model, are elaborated by building up thin washes of blue and flesh tones. Verticals are added to create space and structure (4).

A strong slate blue wash is painted in at the top of the blind with lighter diagonals below, forcing the light through the lower half of the window. Broad areas of cadmium orange are applied to establish the body and the vermilion skirt begins to appear (5).

Forms are made solid in space.
Thin black vertical and diagonal
lines and a stronger brown one
are added to the blind. The
profile and upper arm are
accentuated and a strong line
traces the contours of the
model's left side. A slate blue
wash forms her shadow while a
blue wash with a striped effect
gives the bed height (6).
Rich strong flesh tones in raw
sienna, plus white in the face,
are applied to the body. The
outstretched leg is modeled, the
white of the paper giving
luminosity (7).
The artist adds gouache white
for highlights (8).
A strong blue gouache wash
used with white establishes the
bed. Further shadow is built up
and deep pink flesh tones added
to strengthen the body's
modeling. More vermilion and a
streak of lemon are added to the
skirt (9).

DRAWING THE FIGURE

Characteristics of Drawing

The dictionary defines drawing as the art of making pictures with pencil or pen and ink. This is a perfectly adequate explanation, but drawing can be both much simpler and much more complicated than that. Any mark, made deliberately onto a flat surface, even if it is only a line drawn into sand with the finger, can be described as drawing. At the same time, the distinction between drawing and painting is not always clear. As a general guide, drawing can be distinguished from painting because the former is primarily concerned with line while the latter has more to do with tone and color, even though many drawings contain elements of all three. A painting, however, often makes use of tone, color and form to create a total illusion; to make the viewer believe, momentarily, that the frame of the painting is a window through which the painted scene can be observed as if it existed in reality. A drawing is much more a statement about reality than it is an attempt to copy it. Although an artist may represent three dimensions in a drawing by using solid modeling, many drawings are nothing more than a simple outline which separates one area of the paper from the next. The space defined and enclosed by line in some mysterious way takes on a dynamism of its own; existing in a self-imposed context.

While it is this linear quality which helps to distinguish drawing from painting, the line also distinguishes drawing from reality. In real life nothing has a line drawn around it. Things can be perceived because they are made up of solid, light-reflecting masses. Their apparent outlines change as either they, or the viewer, move from place to place. The drawn line is a visual symbol, standing for the difference between a solid shape and the space surrounding it. It is not the line which receives attention, but the shape of the space or mass which it implies. Even so, the line does have a quality of its own and this inevitably influences the feeling of the drawing. Paul Klee (1879-1940) talked of "taking a line for a walk" and was very aware of its intrinsic energy. By experimenting with different drawing media it can soon be seen that even an abstract line has a character of its own. A line drawn with a stick of charcoal will have a vigor and urgency that cannot be suggested by a delicate pencil.

Most people see drawing as a form of visual record or a type of documentary. This categorization encompasses everything from the briefest of sketches, intended only to note an idea for later development, to finished studies. Michelangelo made hundreds of drawings to investigate the figure in different positions and from different angles. Despite the fact that these drawings were part of the process of painting and sculpting, they are also works of art in themselves. Similarly, Rembrandt, Rubens, Raphael, and many others made numerous studies of the head. While these may have been made with particular paintings in mind, the studies demonstrate powerful artistic curiosity. This type of drawing is a way of finding things out, of seeing how they look, of discovering how the quality and intensity of a line can be used to interpret the texture of surfaces.

However, in order to understand more about the nature and power of the line, it is worth examining different types of drawing where the line takes on a special significance beyond its capacity to define forms in space. Cave drawings, picture languages and the stylized drawing of children all help to demonstrate the more expressive aspects of the line.

The oldest works of art which survive are drawings. Examples in France and Spain, dating back to the paleolithic period, include animal figures drawn onto the walls of caves. These drawings were probably made with lumps of earth or clay which may have contained traces of minerals such as iron oxide or may have been burnt to enrich the color. The exact purpose of these drawings is not known, but it is assumed that they were part of the ritual of the hunt and it has been suggested that by marking the image of a creature on the wall, primitive people felt that they had gained power over the beast or tamed it in some way.

Drawing has also played a large part in the development of the written language. Some scripts today, such as Chinese, still retain a pictorial quality. Early writings, such as Ancient Egyptian hieroglyphics, closely resemble strip cartoons. The Egyptians made little distinction between their paintings, which were really colored drawings, and writing. The purpose of their tomb paintings was to convey information, not to create the illusion of reality. Egyptian sculpture and some of the less formal paintings show that they were quite capable of imitating real life, but this was not their principal intention.

In the light of these "primitive" examples, it is interesting to trace the development of drawing ability in children. When infants first begin to express themselves using paper and pencil there are certain typical stages through which they pass. The basic urge to draw appears to be instinctive; children with no paper or pencil will use sticks and stones to scratch marks on the ground. Not until they are much older does it occur to them that the marks they make should bear any resemblance to reality: a young child draws simply to make a statement. Nevertheless, children are selective and everything that is represented has a special significance.

Many studies have been made of the early years of a child's development and it has been suggested that the first thing a child learns to distinguish is the face of its mother. Later, the overwhelming fascination of this face is represented in simple terms when the child begins to draw. First pictures of "Mother" often consist of a large circle containing smaller circles indicating eyes and mouth.

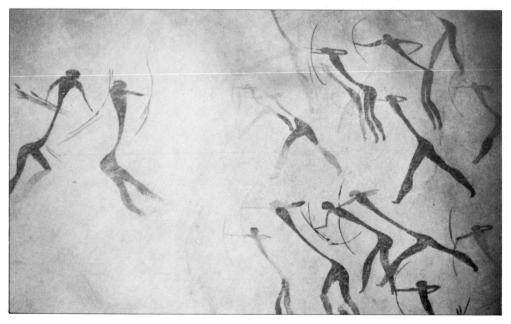

Children's drawings
Drawing is the child's first artistic creation and is his instinctive response to the visual world. His first visual reality will therefore be his mother's face, and as this two-year-old's drawing shows, the eyes and nose are of particular significance. Single lines are used to represent the legs and feet (1).
As the child's visual and mental perception develops, so does his ability to note down what he sees. This drawing by a five-year-old includes more details. Note the preoccupation with the hands, particularly the differentiation between the thumb and fingers (2). The awareness of his hands is probably due to the fact that children of this age learn many new manual skills, particularly writing.

1

3

This drawing by a child of two and half years shows the figure contained in a mandala form, the age-old instinctive way of representing the human figure, perhaps a security motif. The child has balanced the design by adding arbitrary squiggles (3). The more developed drawing,

by a thirteen-year-old, shows a strong awareness of composition, and an acute observation of everyday things, such as the necklace, lamp and bottom of the table. A good attempt has been made to depict the fingers realistically (4).

4

The power of this image is such that, at this stage, the child will often make no attempt to include the body.

The next typical stage is the drawing of the figure where arms and legs are shown radiating from a circular head. Again, the elements which are included reflect their importance at this point in the child's development. Someone who has only recently learned to walk will be very aware of the function of the legs. The child records this milestone in his development by acknowledging limbs on paper, usually with a single pencil line, but often culminating in big feet. Similarly the hands, over which the child has only imperfect control, may be disproportionately large in his or her drawings.

Like paleolithic man making cave pictures of animals in order to assume control over them, children attempt to reinforce their identities through drawing; in this way, they can exercise control over the environment in the act of recreating it. As children become more aware of surroundings, other elements begin to appear in the drawings. Sky and ground are often represented by two lines, one above and one below the figure. Sometimes a single line is used which completely encloses the figure in a secure mandala, a feature which has been observed in the drawings of children of all races, both primitive and civilized. The implications are fairly obvious: the child is using the line drawn around the figure as a symbol for security, a protection against the unknown.

The way in which children draw figures in action is often interesting. A running figure may be drawn with legs which are no different to those of a standing figure, except for the fact that they are twice the size. In a manner reminiscent of medieval painting, the child is drawing attention to the function of the legs by enlarging them out of proportion to the rest of the body.

It is not always easy to interpret children's drawings except by being present while they are being made. Children usually draw attention to the significance of marks they make, although they may later forget what the marks were supposed to represent. Usually they do not take more than a few minutes to complete each drawing and once it is finished it will be set aside and forgotten. It seems as though the actual process is of far greater importance than the result.

It is only as the child grows older that he begins to want to make drawings which are less subjective and more a literal imitation of the visual world. This comes partly as a result of observations of other people's drawings and paintings. It is also at least partly due to the expectations of adults who will ask, "What is it meant to be?" and will even call upon the child to justify the contents of a picture. It is then that it becomes important that it should fall within the conventions accepted by the adult world. A child who has quite happily portrayed "Mother" with a frizz of red hair when really it is straight and dark will suddenly see the drawing as "wrong". At this stage, the naivety of the child's drawing begins to be replaced by sophistication, but many artists have tried to recover the naive quality of children's drawing in their own work.

Just as when children draw they are not seeking to imitate reality but to say something about it, so artists may choose to concentrate upon a particular aspect of their subject matter. If they are interested in facial expressions then their drawings will not be the same as if they were interested in investigating anatomical features. At its most extreme, this preoccupation leads to exaggerated caricature.

The drawings of George Grosz (1893-1959) are sensitive and emotionally charged representations of some of the less desirable of human characteristics. Nobody would suggest that his drawings attempt to portray

Right *St James Led to his Execution,* Andrea Mantegna (1431-1506). Mantegna first worked in Padua, the center of Humanism in north Italy, which helped to determine his style. His knowledge of classical archaeology led him to depict the human body on a monumental scale, sculpturally modeled with archaeological precision. In this sketch for the destroyed fresco in Padua, the figures are well placed in relation to each other, showing Mantegna's preoccupation with design, and movement is rendered by the strong verticals and diagonals.

these qualities through lifelike imagery. The manic and savage expressions of his characters are conveyed almost entirely by line, the occasional suggestion of tone being incidental to the linear quality. The variety and intensity of the line makes his work very expressive. Grosz people are animalistic in their desires and fears, both of which are nakedly apparent on their faces. Although his drawings are humorous in tone, Grosz illustrates the human condition in a peculiarly realistic way. The fact that this "realism" is not photographic does not in any way detract from the significance of the drawing. In fact, the language chosen to convey this particular message is exact, apt and evocative of the seedy world his characters inhabit.

Drawing is a highly subjective activity; the way in which different people draw is as recognizable as their handwriting. The finished work is partly an objective record of what artists see and partly a record of how they feel about what they saw. This instinctive response to the visual world is as different and various as there are individuals; this is one reason why there is always something new to draw.

Left *Death Cycle: Death Holding a Girl in his Lap* (1934-35), Käthe Kollwitz (1867-1945). In this lithograph, the artist has achieved a marvelous marriage between subject and technique, the sweeps of expressive line and areas of dark, heavy tone creating a strong sense of pathos and compassion. A graphic artist and sculptor, Kollwitz lived in the slums of Berlin and her work displays her concern in emotive line.
Above *Face of a Man*, George Grosz. The apparently simple, fluid lines of this caricature display a consummate knowledge of draftsmanship. Each line is made up of short, broken strokes which imbue the well-observed portrait with energy, and exude Grosz's hatred of the bourgeoisie.

Paper

The choice of drawing materials available to the artist is very wide and an enormous range of effects can be achieved. The first consideration must be the sort of ground which is to be used. Since the time of the first drawings, executed on the walls of caves, man's ingenuity has brought all sorts of improbable surfaces into use. Clay pots, notably those from Ancient Greece and Rome, were a favorite recipient for the drawn mark and today provide evidence of the life of those civilizations. Wood, bark, leaves, papyrus, silk, vellum and parchment were all used as drawing surfaces by primitive peoples. Precious metals, stone, shell and wax tablets all have had designs engraved upon them.

Paper, however, remains the most common choice. It provides a good and regular surface for drawing, is relatively cheap and readily available, and is convenient and easy to transport. Although most drawings are done using a dark line on white or light-colored paper, there is no reason to abide by this convention. It is also possible to make drawings onto dark paper using a variety of implements, such as light-colored pencils, pastels, chalks, crayons or pens with white ink.

Paper has not always been the inexpensive and easily available commodity it is today. The first known use of paper was in China as long ago as the second century A.D. Its use gradually spread through Islam and Byzantium until, by the thirteenth and fourteenth centuries, it was available in certain parts of Europe.

Papermaking was a skilled craft which involved pulping fibers of vegetable origin in water, which was sometimes mixed with some form of adhesive binder. The fibers were collected on a perforated frame and then allowed to dry. It is only comparatively recently that wood-pulp has replaced other vegetable fibers to become the most commonly used ingredient in papermaking. More expensive paper is still manufactured from fine linen or cotton rag, and silk and rice paper continue to be made, mostly in Japan and China.

Paper is available from stationers and art suppliers in standardized sizes and a variety of weights and surface textures. The old paper sizes, now partly replaced by A sizes, were Demy (20 × 15½ inches), Medium (22 × 17½ inches), Royal (24 × 19 inches), Imperial (30 × 20 inches), Double Elephant (40 × 26¾ inches) and the enormous Antiquarian (53 × 31 inches). With the new system of A sizes, each measure is half as much again as that of the previous one. The categories range from AO (841 × 1189 mm), through the popular A4 size (210 × 297 mm) to A10 (26 × 37 mm). This means that although paper sizes may vary, proportions are always the same. Some people might consider this a disadvantage. There is no reason for the artist to accept these standard sizes and formats as they are. It may be that a particular subject would be better drawn on a piece of paper that was more square in proportion or more oblong. Large sheets of paper can easily be cut down into a number of smaller ones offering a variety of formats.

The three most commonly available paper surfaces are: Hot Pressed or HP, which is smooth and shiny; Cold Pressed or Not (meaning *not* Hot Pressed) which has a medium smooth texture; and Rough, which is often handmade and preserves the natural, granular surface. Today, paper is usually bleached or artificially colored and fillers such as chalk are used to improve the surface. Hot Pressed paper is ideal for drawing in pen and ink because its smooth surface allows the pen strokes to move across the paper without impediment. For pencil work, the slightly rougher texture of Cold Pressed paper is usually considered to be preferable, while the surface of Rough paper is at its best when used for the broader strokes of chalk or charcoal.

Although paper is a fairly cheap material, particularly in relation to the other types of surface, the price and quality can vary a good deal. Cheaper paper is perfectly acceptable for everyday use, but bears no relation to the quality of good handmade paper, which is naturally much more expensive. Many qualities of paper come in a choice of shade and color, with quite a wide range available. The choice will depend very much upon the sort of drawing to be done. A drawing which emphasizes linear aspects or dwells upon detail would be better on a white or pale neutral paper. Tinted papers are best used for tonal drawings as this will allow both the light and dark areas to be positively defined against the mid-tone of the paper. Some draftsmen respond better to one type of paper than another. Experimenting with different types of paper is well worth the effort and time.

For a pen and wash or a watercolor drawing it is often better to stretch the paper. This is done by soaking the paper for a short time in cold water and then attaching it to a drawing board with thumb tacks or gummed paper strips. As the paper dries it acquires a taut, drum-like surface which is pleasant for drawing on and does not wrinkle when wet paint or ink is applied.

Media

Charcoal

One primitive drawing implement which is still popular today is charcoal. In earlier times, stubs of charred wood would have

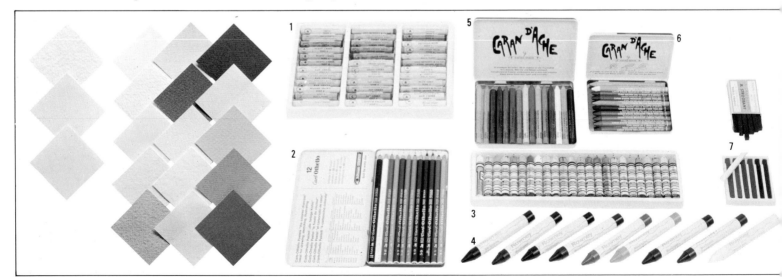

6

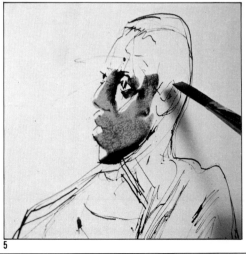

5

Using a small flat brush the first wash is laid over the face, carefully describing the shadowed parts and avoiding thin areas left white to bring out the volumes of the lips, chin and nose, and the circle of the eye-socket. It is possible to take out the intensity of a wash using a sponge to soak up excess ink. The artist leaves thin, dark areas under the brow, down the side of the nose and under the ear to describe shadow and form; the rest of the face is painted in a flat tone to give an impression of the color of the skin (5).

Thin washes are laid over the whole figure to bring out the form almost in an abstract way. The shadowed parts of the body are filled in straight, flat stripes; the upper left arm, being in shadow, is completely blocked in. At the same time, the artist changes his position, moving further round to the front of the model. As a result, the position of the right arm is moved out from the body, the elbow creating more of an angle. The neck and collarbone are carefully detailed at this stage, with brushed ink describing the

directions of the neck and chest muscles, and also describing the flesh wrinkling over the abdomen (6).

The artist's new position is further to the front of the model (7). The detail (8) shows the artist using a sponge to make wide, flat stripes in the thick ink wash to describe shadows on the figure and the sofa. The ink is well diluted but, despite this, the outline drawing beneath, which has previously soaked into the paper and dried, does not run.

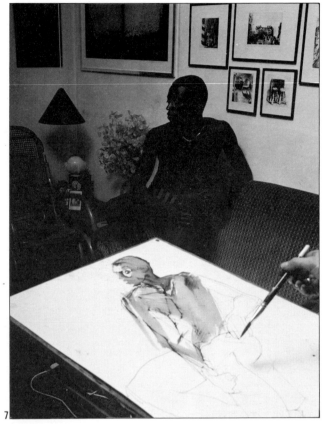

Working on shadows and highlights, the artist continues blocking in areas of darker ink, sometimes on wet patches of paper deliberately to cause the outlines to blur, then allows the washes to dry. The hair is carefully worked to look curly against the white background (9). Lights are emphasized by adding strong black areas of shadow in juxtaposition, down the front of the left shin, for example. The blurred outlines are firmed, details such as the ear added and the background filled in with thin washes (10).

118

Making such a detailed and well-formed picture in ink washes is a slow-moving process, because of the need to wait for the ink to dry at various stages. The final image displays a depth and roundness which can only be achieved by the careful working and over-laying of washes. The figure is drawn and almost completely filled with various shades of grey and some black, which indicate the model's dark skin. The form of the figure is indicated by the intricate and varied shadows; the highlights, in thin tones which allow the white of the paper to show through, add interest and vitality to the picture. The technique works well, describing the directions and shapes of muscles, and directions of tension within the figure in the built-up tones, which seem to have been nonchalently laid and match the mood of the subject, but which describe the figure accurately and with great energy (11).

11

GIRL IN WAISTCOAT

monoprint and pastel on paper 25½ × 20 inches (65 × 51 cm)

Printmaking usually involves making an edition of near-identical images from one plate or block. The exception is the monoprint, which is a print in that the picture is made on another surface and transferred to the support, but it is a once-only image. It involves removing ink from an inked plate by drawing with a stick, a pen or a brush, and placing the paper to take the image over the top.

Monoprints are sometimes used as a basis over which elaborations of color or incised drawing can be added. Edgar Degas reinforced some of his with pastel drawing. Monoprinting is often considered the most immediate means of drawing, enabling the artist to work with the kind of freedom normally associated with oil paint, and the flexibility of the technique allows considerable alteration to be made while drawing is in progress. It is particularly suited to representing strong tonal contrasts.

The model is seated at the end of a bed, with her legs stretched out to one side of her, down the side of the bed. It is a relaxed and casual pose, although the face is angled at the viewer who is asked to meet her level gaze. The lines of the pose are straightforward and uncomplicated; there are no overwhelming problems of foreshortening or complex anatomical demands. The model is well-built and fleshy; the curves of her stomach and thighs provide interesting volumes for the artist. The light is coming into the room from the model's righthand side, and highlights are clearly visible on her right hand, her stomach, right shin and over the thighs and the right side of her face. The leather waistcoat also reflects streaks of light. The artist deliberately chooses an article which enables him to exploit the medium (1).

Linseed oil is added to some black lithographic ink to thin the ink and make it less sticky. Only a small amount of ink is required and it is mixed with the oil until the substance is creamy. The artist applies the ink to a sheet of formica using a roller. Sometimes glass or copper or zinc plates are used. The method works as long as the surface is smooth and completely non-absorbent (2). The drawing process begins. A broad brush and a rag are used to remove ink from areas of the formica. A rag can be used to remove solid areas of ink, which will indicate whole areas of light. Starting with the head, the artist works over the whole area, indicating the basic position of the figure (3). A variety of brushes are employed, for marks of different sizes and shapes; these will give the impression of different textures. If a mistake is made, it is possible to replace the ink and start again. Otherwise, ink can be removed in an area, then some can be brushed back to create marks within the highlight (4).

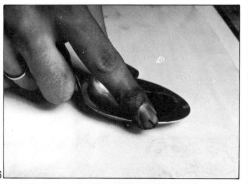

6

7

The basic drawing reaches a state of completion; the form of the figure is established and the background a uniform black. The highlights look over-stated at this stage, but the artist is anticipating working over the print with pastels (5). The formica is placed flat on the floor and a piece of smooth cartridge paper laid over the top. The image would emerge less distinctly if it were pressed to a coarse-grained paper. Using the back of the spoon (6) and the pressure of hands, ink is forced from the formica into the paper. The more pressure applied while burnishing, the denser the image. The small point of contact that a spoon makes creates a thin streakiness, as can be seen over the background. The artist choses to work the spoon over the paper using a criss-cross pattern (7).

5

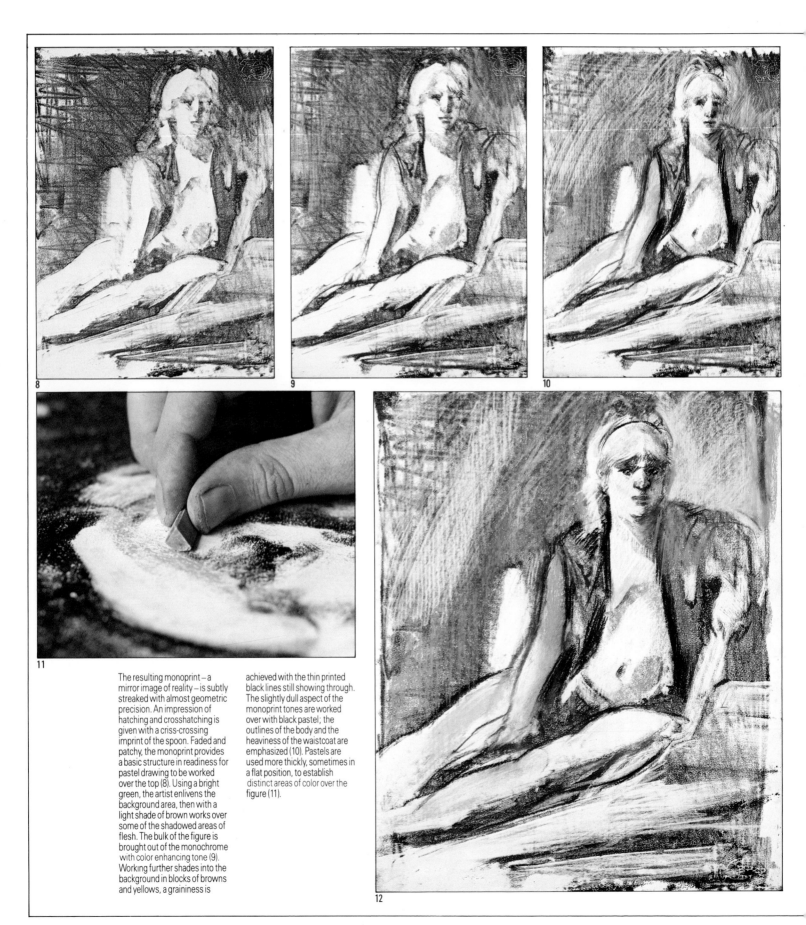

8

9

10

11

The resulting monoprint – a mirror image of reality – is subtly streaked with almost geometric precision. An impression of hatching and crosshatching is given with a criss-crossing imprint of the spoon. Faded and patchy, the monoprint provides a basic structure in readiness for pastel drawing to be worked over the top (8). Using a bright green, the artist enlivens the background area, then with a light shade of brown works over some of the shadowed areas of flesh. The bulk of the figure is brought out of the monochrome with color enhancing tone (9). Working further shades into the background in blocks of browns and yellows, a graininess is achieved with the thin printed black lines still showing through. The slightly dull aspect of the monoprint tones are worked over with black pastel; the outlines of the body and the heaviness of the waistcoat are emphasized (10). Pastels are used more thickly, sometimes in a flat position, to establish distinct areas of color over the figure (11).

12

A strong rust-red pastel is used to block in areas of shadow and add some richer flesh tones. The white of the unprinted paper still shows through, but the effect is more solid than the graininess of the background. Detail is added to the face, and white highlights bring out the volume against the darks (12). The artist decides in this final stage to change the model's pose slightly. This last-minute decision illustrates the way pastel can be used as an opaque medium. To give some balance to the pose, and break the strong, curving diagonal of the body, the elbow is moved out using highlights to cover the shape beneath. The right hand and fingers are detailed over the strong lines of the model's left thigh, white and cream pastel covering the black, reds and browns underneath. Although pastel is generally considered to be a transparent, luminous medium, it also has a covering potential, which is fully exploited here (13).

13

RECLINING MALE FIGURE
charcoal on paper 20 × 37½ inches (51 × 95 cm)

1

For any artist familiar with the use of a pencil, the prospect of drawing with charcoal can be slightly daunting. Even the softest pencil allows for precision and control and enables the artist to follow sinuous contours with a certain amount of ease. Charcoal is more abrasive and dramatic and should be used with less concern for sharp definition. Available either in pencil form or in the traditional sticks of varying thicknesses, it can be applied in broad areas, smudged to achieve blurred effects, and fixed at intervals to maintain its richness.

For this drawing a grey-green paper was chosen, which provided a mid-tone ground. Papers in dark colors and mid-tones, which can be bought or otherwise made by laying a watercolor wash and allowing it to dry before beginning work, are sometimes chosen so that the artist can "work to the lights". A feeling of volume is often more apparent if white chalk is added for the highlights after the drawing has been established in charcoal.

Occasionally the size of the paper proves inadequate as the drawing progresses. In this case the drawing was extended by adding an extra piece of paper to the lefthand side of the drawing to accommodate the legs.

Although a reclining pose is often suggestive of ease and relaxation, this need not always be the case. Here, the slightly uncomfortable position of the male figure exhibits a certain tension, the clasped right hand and angled shoulders implying a latent energy in the form. Attention is directed to the sharp angles and strong shadows, an interest which demands a forceful and immediate treatment. Charcoal is the chosen medium for this drawing, being more direct and less hesitant than pencil. The artist intends to make the figure occupy most of the paper area and has discounted the surrounding area. Only a slight reference is made to context, enough to establish the position of the figure in space, but not detract from it (1).

2

3

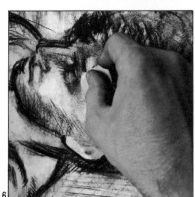

4

Using a linear approach, the artist begins the drawing by concentrating on the head and upper torso, roughly sketching in the main outlines and contours lightly, to allow for redefinition (2). Moving across the paper, more detail is added to the face and hair. The artist uses a putty eraser to remove some of the initial lines; the position of the left arm is redrawn and a greater emphasis is placed on the sharp angle it makes. Some shading is added, but the main concern at this stage is to establish the crucial angles of the head, shoulders and arms (3). Light hatching on the shoulders, neck and torso begin to suggest volume; heavier lines behind the figure fill in the shadow areas (4). A slight movement of the model's head calls for small adjustments to be made to the

5

6

7

drawing. The artist again uses a putty eraser to make these alterations, restating the hair (5). Putty erasers are more suitable for erasing charcoal lines than hard erasers. They are soft and can be molded to a point to take out small details or make highlights, or they can lighten an area by a tone without smearing (6). The drawing has been executed on handmade paper with a slight grain, suitable for charcoal. It is grey-green in color, establishing a mid-tone ground. Highlights are added with white chalk to reinforce the sense of volume in the figure. Adding highlights to a toned ground, rather than using a stark white paper, is the traditional method of working (7).

Although the addition of high-lighting in white chalk has virtually completed the drawing, the artist is dissatisfied with the result (8). As happens quite frequently, especially when making preparatory studies for further work in another medium, the paper's format and the composition look wrong. The artist decides to add more paper to the lefthand side of this drawing to accommodate a representation of the legs of the figure. Once this has been accomplished and the extended drawing is completed, the benefits become obvious. The shaded area of the legs balance the detail and definition of the head and make sense of the pose. Such alterations are part of a process of investigation and discovery (9).

PAINTING THE FIGURE

Painting, like drawing, is the enclosing of a view of three-dimensional reality in two dimensions. The difference between the two techniques is that drawing is concerned with the use of line to convey the solidity of form, whereas painting is generally more concerned with the use of tone and color to convey not only form but the qualities of light. Finished paintings are also more likely to give a complete picture, whether realistic or symbolic, because the whole surface is usually covered.

Color and Pigment

An understanding of color and the effects of color in different combinations is important before an artist can hope to paint in the way he or she intends. Often this understanding is gained through experience in using pigments, but it is worth becoming familiar with basic color theory. Color can vary in three ways: there can be differences of tone, which is the lightness or darkness of a color; there can be differences in hue, which is the quality that distinguishes red from blue or green, for example; and there can be differences in intensity of color, which is the purity or saturation value of the hue. All these can be used with different effects in painting.

The three primary colors, red, blue and yellow, are the only colors that cannot be produced by blending and which, in various combinations, mix to form all the others. The complementary color of each primary is the secondary color made by mixing the other two primaries. So, green, which is made from a mixture of blue and yellow, is the complementary of red; purple is the complementary of yellow; orange is the complementary of blue. Tertiary colors are those which are arrived at by mixing a primary

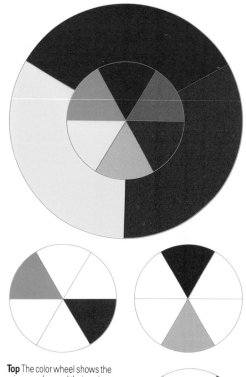

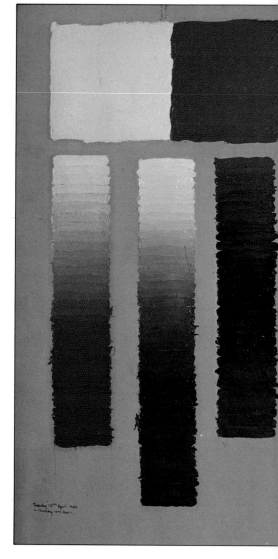

Top The color wheel shows the primary colors and their main gradations. Each color has three independent variations which are tone, brightness and hue. When mixed, the three primary colors on the outer circle, red, blue and yellow, form the secondary colors of green, violet and orange in the inner circle. In 1672, the English scientist, Sir Isaac Newton (1642-1727) discovered that a beam of white light could be split by a triangular prism into its component chromatic rays; he named the seven divisions of color – red, orange, yellow, green, blue, indigo and violet.
Above Complementary colors are those from opposite sides of the color wheel, and they have no primary colors in common.

Pigment sources
Artists' pigments were made from natural or readily accessible substances until the early nineteenth century when the rapidly developing chemical and dyeing industries led to a burst of brilliant new colors. Charcoal (1) yielded black, earth (2) produced various browns and chalk (3) white. Cinnabar (4), realgar (5), malachite (6), orpiment (9), azurite (11), naturally-occurring minerals ground into powder by the Bronze Age Egyptians, produced vermilion, orange, green, yellow and blue. The Romans developed Tyrian purple from whelks (7) and the blue-green color known as verdigris from corroded copper (8). From lapis lazuli (10) came ultramarine, one of the popular colors in the Middle Ages.

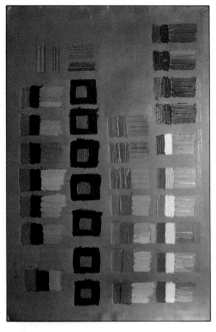

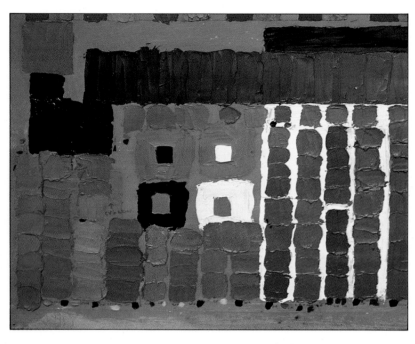

Left Primary colors are so called as they cannot be made by mixing; however, all other colors can be produced by mixing them, either physically or optically. To experiment with the range of hues between the colors is a useful exercise.
Above Secondary colors, orange, purple and green, produce greys when they are mixed together. By combining secondaries or complementaries a wide range of broken colors can be made; these tend to be closest to the colors of nature.
Above right This range of neutral greys gives an idea of how many hues are easily obtained.

color with one of its own secondaries. Blue mixed with green gives turquoise, for example. A color wheel is simple to make and quickly gives information about complementaries, when required.

The Impressionist painters were particularly interested in the effects of light and color and were fascinated to find that the shadow of any given color produced its own complementary. They banished black from their palettes and concentrated on painting in a way which gave the impression of real light, hence their name. More recent artists have experimented with the optical effects of juxtaposing colors which clash or argue with one another, as happens, for instance, with

certain reds and greens. Medieval artists often used color symbolically. For instance, blue and gold were considered to be the colors of eternity. Color is usually used subjectively, and many artists are recognizable for the use of particular color ranges in their paintings.

The paints used by artists to convey color have two main ingredients: finely ground pigment and some form of binding medium. The chosen medium dictates the painting technique to be used in applying the color to the surface. There is a very wide range of pigments available today; most of the paints and colored pencils or pastels in current use are made from pigments which have only been discovered within the last 200 years. This fact has been of considerable assistance when verifying the dates of paintings and drawings, and many forgeries have been uncovered by the detection of modern pigments.

In the past, the range of pigments has been very limited. The roughly prepared earth pigments of cave paintings, for example, which were probably bound with some sort of animal glue, afforded the early artist a palette consisting of only browns and ochers. To this was added a black made from carbonized organic matter. Because of the conditions under which these paintings were executed, it is unlikely that any attempts were made to expand this color range.

By the time of the Egyptian civilization, there were several more pigments available to decorate the walls of the tombs. Their paintings include a delicate yellow which was often used as a background color; this is probably the color we know as Naples

yellow, made from lead antimonate. Terre verte, which literally means "green earth", and malachite, which is a natural, basic copper carbonate, provided them with a choice of greens. Their brown pigments included raw and burnt umber (iron hydroxide and manganese oxide) and cappagh and Verona brown which are natural earth colors. Like the cave painters, the Egyptians used carbonized organic matter for black.

The range of pigments in use in the Middle Ages had extended to include burnt sienna, which is calcined iron and manganese oxide. Around A.D.1400, flake white, or white lead, came into use and despite its disadvantages has been an important component in the artist's palette ever since. Besides being poisonous, this basic lead carbonate tends to darken when exposed to hydrogen sulfide. Many poisonous colors or fugitive colors used in earlier times, including verdigris, orpiment, realgar, massicot yellows, minium and several red lakes, have now become obsolete and have been replaced by more reliable, modern pigments.

It is always worth ascertaining the qualities of each pigment before starting to paint; even now, relatively few pigments are fully permanent and safe to mix with all the others. A pigment's mixing capabilities, its transparency or brilliancy, its consistency when mixed and its drying time are all discovered by experience; whether it is "permanent" or "fugitive" and, if applicable, "toxic" is marked on the label by the maker. The latter description need not deter the artist; it is no more than a warning.

About 60 different pigments are now easily available; a decision to limit the palette is important as a choice of too many colors can be confusing and will not lead to a full understanding of the potentialities of each pigment. An exception to this would be if an artist wishes to emphasize brilliance of color above everything else, because colors made by mixing are slightly denser. A simple palette of warm and cool permanent colors might consist of: flake or titanium white (not needed for watercolor), lemon yellow, yellow ocher, light red, Indian red, raw umber, terre verte, viridian and cobalt blue. Cadmium yellow could be used if a stronger yellow is required; cadmium red, vermilion or alizarin crimson if a brighter red is required. Raw and burnt sienna, French ultramarine and Hooker's green are also useful. These additions are all reasonably permanent if protected from a strong light. Instead of using black, which tends to make colors dull, it is usually better to mix dark colors using, for example, a blue with burnt sienna or raw umber; this principle inspires the artist to discover the true nature of shadows. Endless color variations are possible with just a small selection of pigments, which, in any case, will demand extensive experimentation before the required color is achieved whenever desired, and before the properties of each pigment are understood.

Pigments themselves were traditionally ground by the artist, which was a time-consuming and arduous occupation. Part of an artist's training in previous centuries involved learning how to prepare his own paints and materials; in the Renaissance workshops this job was given to the young apprentices. The more finely the pigment is ground, the better the finished product. The main reason for the disparity in price today between paints described as being for artists and those for students is that the former are more finely ground. Pigments which have not been properly ground produce paints which are patchy in color, particularly apparent in thin washes. Another reason for paints being expensive is costly raw materials; pure ultramarine, for example, is made from ground lapis lazuli.

Media and Techniques

In the past, the varied methods of using the pigments and the different techniques of application have been influenced by the binding medium or vehicle with which they have been mixed. Egyptian and Assyrian painters mixed dry pigments with glue or gum to make paints which they used for decorating both the insides and outsides of their buildings. In the Orient, water-soluble gum or eggwhite was used for painting miniatures, and size, which is a thin liquid glue, for paintings on either paper or silk.

During the first few centuries A.D. the Egyptians, Greeks and Romans made use of beeswax as a medium for encaustic painting. This technique of painting involves fixing the colors by heat, and the results are particularly durable. Great practical problems occurred in its application, however, because the paint only remained fluid enough to work for a short time, even when the palette was kept over a fire and the paint applied with warmed instruments. The technique did not lend itself readily to much elaboration or refinement. Surviving examples of the use of this technique in Egypt, mainly portraits in tombs, have a rough finish showing traces of the instruments used to apply the paint. Some of the wall paintings found in Pompeii and Herculaneum are also thought to be examples of the encaustic method although their surfaces are smooth.

Left *Portrait of a Man and Wife.* The idea of a portrait did not occur to the Greeks until the end of the fourth century B.C. Sculptors had previously represented the ideal man, his face without a particular expression, but around the time of Alexander the Great, they began to invest their portraits with individual characterization. Pompeii, a Roman town, contained reflections of Hellenistic art; Greek artists were employed there, but it was the Roman and Italian painters who developed the Pompeian realistic genre. In this extremely expressive and true-to-life double funeral portrait, the colors are laid on flat, within contours which have been well defined.

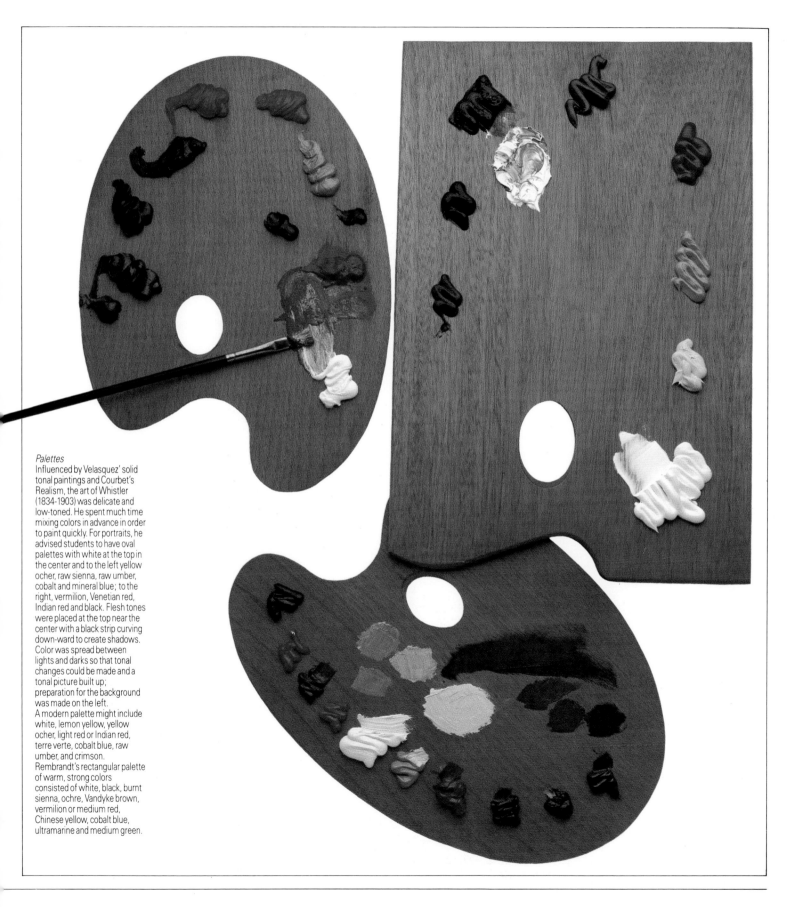

Palettes
Influenced by Velasquez' solid tonal paintings and Courbet's Realism, the art of Whistler (1834-1903) was delicate and low-toned. He spent much time mixing colors in advance in order to paint quickly. For portraits, he advised students to have oval palettes with white at the top in the center and to the left yellow ocher, raw sienna, raw umber, cobalt and mineral blue; to the right, vermilion, Venetian red, Indian red and black. Flesh tones were placed at the top near the center with a black strip curving down-ward to create shadows. Color was spread between lights and darks so that tonal changes could be made and a tonal picture built up; preparation for the background was made on the left.
A modern palette might include white, lemon yellow, yellow ocher, light red or Indian red, terre verte, cobalt blue, raw umber, and crimson.
Rembrandt's rectangular palette of warm, strong colors consisted of white, black, burnt sienna, ochre, Vandyke brown, vermilion or medium red, Chinese yellow, cobalt blue, ultramarine and medium green.

Fresco

Fresco was the first important and popular technique used in applying paint to a background. Both Vitruvius and Pliny (*c.* A.D.23-79) make reference to it in their writings but it was not until the thirteenth century that it came to be widely used across Europe. It is the only method of painting which can truly be termed "watercolor" as it is the only one to use just water as the vehicle for the pigment. It is, however, called "fresco" painting because it involved the application of pigment to fresh plaster. As the plaster dried, the color was bonded into it and became a part of the wall, instead of lying separately on the surface. This made it a particularly durable method.

Because the paint had to be applied while the plaster was still wet, the design of the intended painting had to be planned in sections, each one representing a day's work, and carefully drawn out on paper beforehand. At the beginning of each day, exactly the right area of wall was covered in fresh plaster. Giorgio Vasari, the sixteenth-century artist, architect and biographer, gave fresco his highest accolade, describing it in *Lives of the Most Excellent Painters, Sculptors and Architects* (first published in 1550) as being "the most masterly and beautiful" of methods. He explained how the technique was employed:

"It is worked on the plaster while it is fresh and must not be left until the day's portion is finished. The reason is that if there is any delay in painting, the plaster forms a certain

Above *St Francis Preaching* (1297-*c.*1305), Giotto. Giotto's ability to represent the human figure and emotions and to recreate the visible world on the two-dimensional plane is well demonstrated in this fresco scene.

Left *The Annunciation*, Fra Angelico (*c.*1387-*c.*1455). This fresco, with its perfect sense of color and composition, shows Angelico's interest in perspective to create a harmonious setting for his figures.

Right *Virgin Annunciate* (1527-8), Jacopo Pontormo (1494-1557). Pontormo's works are often exaggerated in form and emotional content. Here he combines high tonality and shot colors to create the Virgin's graceful figure.

Far right *The Delphic Sybil* (detail), Michelangelo Buonarotti. Michelangelo worked on the Sistine ceiling between 1508 and 1512. The Sybil's head and eyes turn away from the movement of her arms, her strong body and face derived from classical sculpture.

slight crust whether from heat or cold or currents of air or frost, whereby the whole work is stained and grows moldy. To prevent this, the wall that is to be painted must be kept continually moist, and the colors employed thereon must all be of earths and not metallic and the white of calcined travertine. There is needed also a hand that is dextrous, resolute and rapid, but most of all a sound and perfect judgement; because while the wall is wet the colors show up in one fashion and afterward when dry they are no longer the same. Therefore in these works done in fresco it is necessary that the judgement of the painter should play a more important part than his drawing and that he should have for his guide the very greatest experience, it being supremely difficult to bring fresco work to perfection."

The colors used for fresco work were almost entirely earth colors, most vegetable and metallic pigments being chemically unsuitable. The "white of calcined travertine" to which Vasari refers, had to be used because the more usual lead white, "biacca", was incompatible. Travertine was a building material widely employed by the Romans, a notable example of its use being the Colosseum. By burning travertine, a white lime appears from which the fresco white "bianco Sangiovanni" was manufactured. As the surface of the painted plaster dried, a chemical reaction caused a crystalline skin of carbonate of lime to form on the surface. This not only protects fresco paintings from damp and other atmospheric conditions but also lends them a metallic luster which is part of their unique appeal.

The limitations of this technique are paradoxically also the reasons for high standards being achieved in its use. The practitioners of fresco painting were obliged to give careful consideration to the planning of the composition, which gave an overall unity of style to each. Also, working against the clock, the frescoer was required to paint deftly and with a sureness of touch. There was no time for corrections, and although details could be added after the work was dry ("fresco-secco") this was not advocated by purists. Additions were sometimes made in tempera paint but this tended to darken quickly and spoil the fresco. Vasari pointed out that it was necessary to "... work boldly in fresco and not retouch it in the dry because, besides being a very poor thing in itself, it renders the life of the picture short".

The most common method of transferring the design to the plaster on the wall involved preparing a full-sized cartoon on paper, then pricking tiny holes along the drawn lines on the cartoon. The paper was then held against the surface to be painted, and a muslin bag containing powdered charcoal was dabbed onto the cartoon so that the design showed up on the plaster as a series of black dots.

Tempera

Painting in the tempera medium has a longer history than fresco painting. The word "tempera" comes from the Latin verb "temperare" which means "to divide or proportion duly; to qualify by mixing; to regulate; to discipline". The literal translation seems appropriate; the mixture of pigment and medium is difficult, needing precision, and the method of applying tempera paint to a ground is itself a discipline. The method has been widely used both in the Orient and in Europe from the earliest times and was extremely popular through the Middle Ages to the fifteenth century, when it was superseded by oil painting. Occasional revivals of interest in this technique have kept it alive until the present day, although it is no longer widely popular.

The normal ground for tempera painting was a wooden panel which was occasionally covered with canvas. The choice of wood varied according to availability. In Italy, poplar was most commonly used, as recommended by the Italian artist and writer Cennini (born c.1370); in central Europe the choice was pine, while in Flanders and northern Europe it was oak. Other woods, including larch, maple, box, lime, fir and willow were also used. The wood had to be well seasoned, planed and, if necessary, jointed. The practice of covering panels with canvas or linen was to prevent joints opening later and spoiling the picture. Next, several layers of gesso ground, the main ingredients of which were size and some form of whitening agent, usually plaster of Paris, were laid over the panel. The gesso was sanded down after it had dried to provide an even, smooth surface on which to work. Sometimes the gesso ground was toned by a coat of resin or size with an added coloring agent, although it was more usual to retain the white surface which reflected light back through the translucent paint, adding brilliance and depth to the color.

A number of different media are favored by different people as the best vehicle for the

Right *The Boxers*. This modern painting shows the effectiveness of large blocks of tempera color combined with acrylic.
Below Looking from left to right, different consistencies can be seen. A directly applied and unworked pure egg tempera is similar to thickly laid watercolor. Painted in a similar way, an egg yolk, stand oil emulsion and damar varnish resemble a mixture of pure tempera and oil paint, resulting in very dense color. A whole egg mixed with damar varnish and oil of cloves emulsion produces a flat, dense color.
Bottom These illustrations show various egg-oil emulsion mixtures which produce a glossier finish than pure tempera. Looking from left to right the mixtures are: one level teaspoon of linseed oil with one egg yolk; one egg yolk, one level teaspoon of blended stand oil and damar varnish; the yolk and white of an egg blended with a teaspoon of linseed oil added drop by drop, and four drops of white vinegar, all strained; 20 drops of oil of cloves added to one egg and a quarter of the egg's volume of damar varnish.

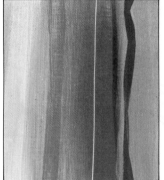

Left *Family and Rainstorm*, David Alexander Colville (b.1920). This painting, on a board support and almost photographic in its treatment of the subject, demonstrates the versatility of tempera, one of the earliest types of paint media. The cool colors, grey, yellow and brown, have a smooth, opaque quality which help to create the sense of stillness and the monumentality of the figures.

pigment in tempera painting. Vasari was firmly of the opinion that the yolk of an egg excelled all others. The following is his description of the way in which the Old Masters prepared tempera paint:

"They whisked up an egg and shredded it into a tender branch of a fig tree, in order that the milk of this with the egg should make the tempera of the colors, which after being mixed with this medium were ready for use. They chose for these panels mineral colors of which some are made by the chemists and some found in the mines. And for this kind of work all pigments are good, except the white used for work on walls made with lime, for that is too strong. In this manner their works and their pictures are executed, and this they call coloring in tempera. But the blues are mixed with parchment size, because the yellow of the egg would turn them green, whereas size does not affect them, nor does gum."

Tempera paint has a number of advantages over fresco painting and many of the great exponents of the latter worked their smaller pieces in tempera. With its brilliant white gesso ground the paint has a greater luminosity than it was possible to achieve in fresco work, and also a slightly greater depth

of tone. Because the paint could be laid in thicker layers, the light areas could be built up more strongly. It was also the practice of artists to create softer transitions of tone by "scumbling". This is the laying of semi-transparent light paint over darker areas, sometimes in an irregular way, to modify the paint beneath by creating areas of broken color. Being a flexible medium, artists were able to include areas of fine elaboration in tempera paintings.

Medieval artists were beginning to establish a method for painting the human figure. Areas which were to be flesh were given an underpainting, usually of terre verte. This subdued green complemented the pinkish color of the flesh and was allowed to shine through in areas of shadow to provide the half-tones. The green underpainting was sometimes heightened by the addition of white and occasionally greater depth was added by shading areas in transparent brown. All this preparatory work was important in helping to give tonal depth to the finished painting and was, interestingly, closer to the ideas of the Impressionists than to the practice of adding black to arrive at darker tones, which was more normal at the time.

After the underpainting, the artist mixed enough of each of the colors he intended to use, to avoid running out before completing a painting. As with fresco, tempera changes as it dries and the colors lighten by several shades. The experienced tempera painter would make allowances for this but it was always difficult to match a new batch of color with any that had already dried. The preparatory mixing partly accounts for the continuity of hue which is noticeable with this method of painting. Three main colors were mixed in order to paint the flesh. The artist began by laying in the main areas with a mid-tone, then worked over the top with the darker then the lighter tones. Later, a semi-transparent mixture of black and yellow ocher called "verdaccio" provided the deepest shadows.

When painting the clothed figure, the system was almost the same as for flesh. The colors for the underpainting were designed to complement whatever colors were chosen to go over the top; red, for example, took a greenish-grey underpaint, and blue usually took a white-grey or occasionally a green. The top color was similarly painted in stages: the mid-tone first, then the darker and then the lighter areas.

Oil

The invention of oil painting is attributed, by Vasari, to Jan van Eyck who was working at the beginning of the fifteenth century. Although oil had been used as a vehicle for pigments by earlier artists, van Eyck was certainly the first artist to develop a recognizable technique of working with pigment suspended in oil. He was the first to exploit the way in which colors could be blended softly to achieve a more natural effect than was possible with tempera. He probably ground his pigments in some sort of refined oil, possibly linseed or walnut oil, which, according to Vasari, is less inclined to darken with age. Because oil paint alone would, it is believed, take about 400 years to dry, it was necessary to add an agent to accelerate this process. Van Eyck probably used turpentine which would have thinned the paint as well as helping it to dry.

The support which is most commonly associated with oil painting is canvas although artists continued to use wooden panels as well. These had originally been used because of their rigidity which was an important consideration when working with a medium such as tempera. With its greater flexibility, oil paint could be applied to a less rigid support without the danger of its cracking. There are obvious advantages in using canvas. It is light, which makes it easier to transport than wood and also allows for larger paintings than had previously been practical. Canvas can be rolled when not in use which makes it economical of space, and it is also more economical to buy than large panels of wood.

The traditional method of preparing a canvas, and one which is popularly used today, is to stretch the canvas over a wooden frame and secure it with tacks. Wooden frames consist of "stretchers" which can be made at home but are also available at art suppliers. The stretchers are jointed at the corners in such a way that the tension of the canvas can be adjusted at a later stage by hammering in wooden pegs. Raw linen is the best material to use and it is easier to stretch if it is slightly dampened first. Once stretched, the surface of the canvas can be prepared for the oil paint. Some of the earlier users of oil paint continued to lay a ground of gesso, but this was not found to be entirely suitable as canvas tends to contract and expand with changing atmospheric conditions, which caused the rigid gesso to crack and flake off. Also, finished canvases were often rolled up for transportation, and a flexible grounding was obviously necessary. The usual method employed by artists today is to give the canvas several coats of size, the purpose of which is to fill the pores of the canvas and make it non-absorbent. There are various

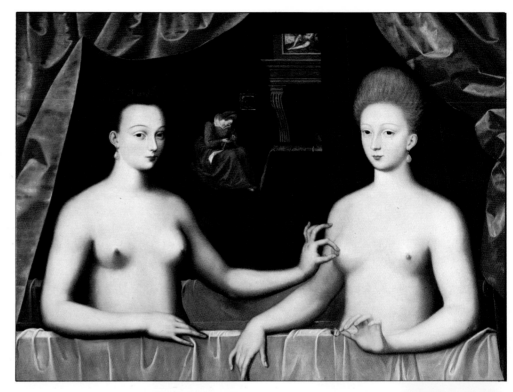

Above *Gabrielle d'Estrées and her Sister,* School of Fontainebleau. This double portrait in oils of the mistress of François I and her sister exemplifies the sensual and decorative style of painting which flourished in France between 1528 and 1558. The rich, glossy qualities of the medium complement the etiolated elegance of the subject.

Right Canvases are usually made from linen, cotton, a linen cotton mixture, and hessian. Unbleached calico is a cheap cotton weave (1). A good cotton canvas is almost as good as linen provided that it has previously been primed (2). Hessian is coarse and needs a good deal of priming (3) while linen (4 and 5) is the best and most expensive type of canvas coming in several weaves, the best of which are closely woven with the threads knot-free. Linen primed with acrylic, is multi-purpose (6).

Right Canvas is the most common support for oil paintings, and is extremely receptive to the paint when fixed to a stretcher. Wood for stretchers comes in many lengths, and pieces can be fitted together to make rectangles of all sizes.

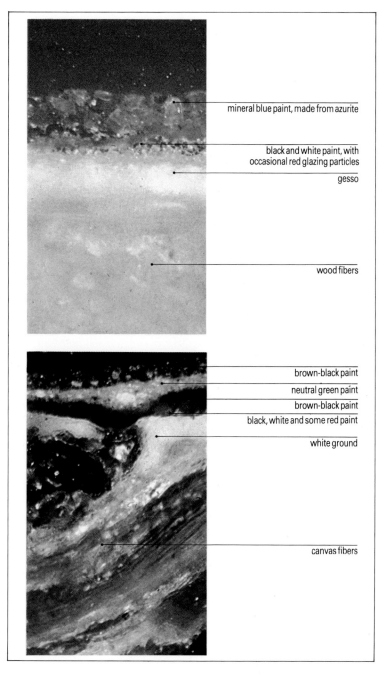

mineral blue paint, made from azurite

black and white paint, with occasional red glazing particles

gesso

wood fibers

brown-black paint
neutral green paint
brown-black paint
black, white and some red paint

white ground

canvas fibers

Left This cross-section of an early Flemish painting has been magnified 200 times. Wood was used as a support for easel paintings by the Egyptians, and again in medieval and early Renaissance art. This cross-section shows the gesso ground, made from plaster mixed with size, and layers of paint.
Below left This cross-section of an early painting by Titian has been magnified 100 times. It was one of the first paintings to be done on canvas. The white ground has penetrated the canvas fibers and the neutral green underpaint, terre verte, applied as a ground for flesh painting, is revealed.
Below *Portrait of a Woman with Gloves and Crossed Hands*, Frans Hals. Chiefly known as a portraitist, Hals was an extremely original artist with a unique directness of approach. Influenced by the Caravaggisti, he used *chiaroscuro* for dramatic effects in rendering instantaneous impressions. Bold brushstrokes and impasto build up textures, particularly evident in the hands.

kinds of size available; rabbit-skin preparations are generally considered to be the best.

The next stage involves covering the surface of the canvas with a "primer" which is prepared from a number of ingredients. Vasari gives a recipe which consists of "a paste made of flour and walnut oil with two or three measures of white lead put into it". The following recipes for grounds are only guidelines and should not be considered as the only possible ones to use; grounds are very much a matter of individual preference.

A simple but efficient oil ground consists of six parts turpentine, one part linseed oil and some flake white. This should be applied to a dry surface which has already received two coats of size, applied when hot. The ground should be brushed on, and left to dry for 24 hours, and then a second coat applied and left for about a month before using. An emulsion ground might be mixed with one part whiting, one part glue size, one part zinc oxide and half part linseed oil. A simple gesso ground, for use on wood or hardboard, might consist of one part whiting and one part size. The dry whiting should be sieved into some of the heated glue size until a smooth paste is achieved. The rest of the hot size should then be mixed in to give the gesso mixture the consistency of cream.

The addition of white clay gives greater body to the ground, while an acrylic medium, a synthetic resin, could be included for its elastic properties. It is a good idea to include an anti-fungus and anti-bacterial agent, which is often added into proprietary brands of glue size as a matter of course.

Several layers of primer should be laid. For the final coat, some artists prefer to add some coloring pigment, thus giving themselves a tinted ground on which to work. Some, preferring to give the surface of the canvas "teeth", dab the heel of the hand against the wet primer. Applying the primer with a foam sponge roller gives a similar effect.

Many of the pigments used today are recent innovations. Artists from previous centuries had very few colors to choose from, but even so they often deliberately worked from a palette with further restrictions self-imposed. Now, with a large range of pigments available, it is more important than before to choose a palette of only a few colors, as this is more likely to result in a unity and harmony being achieved in a painting than when a confusing jumble of pigments are at hand. Also, it means that the artist becomes increasingly familiar with the few chosen colors, and can exploit them to the full.

Because the pigment is suspended in oil, which turns into a solid, transparent substance when dry, a number of glazes need to be laid, one over the other, to achieve the required shades and tones. The layers together combine to give depth to the colors, while they retain a brillance in the transparency. These qualities are enhanced by the use of underpainting. Light reflects back through thin layers of paint from a white or pale underpainting, so giving work an extra luminosity.

The major advantage of oil paint is that it remains workable over a long time, allowing colors to be blended, modified or changed as the work progresses. The oil itself retards the drying time of the paint, while the addition of turpentine or varnish accelerates it. Each subsequent glaze should contain more oil than the previous layer; the last layers need to be well oiled, so that progressive workings retain their elasticity. This means that artists, working from dark to light, can blend highlights carefully and with

as much detail as is required into the hard, dry underlayers without fear of the paints muddying.

The special qualities of oil paint are particularly evident in pictures of the human figure, when they can be exploited to make flesh appear almost translucent, and can be used to express the different textures of cloth very realistically. The medium is also suited to the rendering of mood and emotion, because the paint itself can be varied in texture. The painter can mix it thick or thin, dry or wet, and can either apply it smoothly

so that there is no surface texture and no evidence of manipulation, or roughly, with brushstrokes a definite, stylistic feature. Scumbling, and the techniques of working wet paint into dry, and dry paint into wet are examples of further ways of achieving textured effects and tonal depth. This versatility allows artists to work fluently and expressively within the restrictions of the media, adding their own enthusiasm to the mood of a painting. The variety of techniques can be used in many ways to create vivid representations of nature.

Right *Girl Holding a Fan* (1903), Paul Gauguin. One of the first to find inspiration in the arts of primitive civilizations, he rejected the representational function of color, using it in flat, contrasting areas which strengthened its emotional and decorative effect. He went "native", painting his finest pictures in Tahiti, fascinated by native sculpture and ritual. His forms became more simplified and his colors richer, in tune with with his tropical surroundings. In this oil painting, the strangely represented right arm can be seen as an example of the primitive influence. Using almost flat areas of rich color within strong outlines to form rhythmic patterns, he creates a strong visual image redolent of the nostalgic nineteenth-century idea of the Noble Savage.

GIRL IN CHAIR
acrylic and gouache on paper 21 × 14 inches (53 × 36 cm)

The model is posed beside a window with bright sunlight slanting into the room, creating strong patterns of light and shade over the body (1). The picture artist chooses to ignore the stark contrasts of tone, concentrating instead on the general effects of light. It is interesting to compare the

positions of the shadows in this photograph and in the final picture; in the latter a shadow is delineated over the right thigh in a different position. The picture takes some time to complete, and the artist is always aware of movement, accommodating his painting to it, rather than forcing a rigidity.

Glazing is a method of painting in which thin layers of paint suspended in the sort of medium which allows colors beneath to shine through, are laid one over another. The system of underpainting a monochrome structure and glazing color over the top is part of a long painting tradition. In the past, the common medium for the underpainting was tempera and gouache was used for the glazings. Modern artists have adapted the tradition to accommodate recent developments in materials; acrylics are often used today for the underpainting and gouache

mixed with casein for the glazes. If the underlayer of paint is white, and the glazes semi-transparent, a luminosity and vibrancy is achieved in the harnessing of the priming color; dark or mid-toned underlayers enhance a feeling of depth in the shadows.

The structure of the figure in this painting, which was emphasized by bright, afternoon sunlight, was delineated in firm monochrome strokes. Darks were toned and lights painted in white to give a strong impression of the form of the figure before the gouache was added.

Almost like a sculptor coaxing form from a piece of stone, the artist brings the form of the figure out from the paper by careful modeling. The figure emerges in the building up of a series of monochrome washes in umber on biscuit-colored David Cox watercolor paper. The method is suited to representing subjects or scenes under direct light where volume is emphasized by extremes of light and dark (2 and 3). In the detail, highlights are added in blue and white to give a strong overall structure to the underpainting (4). The background is also laid and blurred streaks of white worked over the model's right shin in preparation for the dark shadows which are to be painted against the bright highlights of that area of the painting (5).

6

8

9

Color is worked over the monochrome structure. Yellows and red-browns are painted over the torso, face and hair, their intensity and tone matching the tones of the underpainting (6). The stomach and breasts are carefully filled with a variety of hues, with a resulting precision of shape and form despite the obvious nature of the brushstrokes (7). Thin and dark, warm patches of brown are laid to delineate the shadows of the thighs, then a series of dark streaks of brown, blue and green are laid to cover the shadowed area of the model's hair and left shoulder (8). The glinting yellow and light brown of the hair beneath is allowed to show in a frame around the face, the rest of the hair looking almost black; this gives a subtle impression of the slanting sunlight. Details of the hands, shins and feet, and the features of the face, are added. With the chair and background also filled, using fingers to smudge the colors the picture gains overall shape (9).

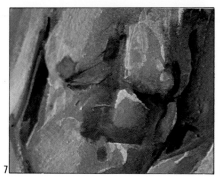

7

Some lights are added; some show through from the underpainting. Over the stomach, breasts, face and hair, extra highlights are painted where sunlight glints over the flesh; the rounded volumes of the figure, however, are mostly achieved in the actual process of underpainting and glazing. The casein medium with gouache allows for a great spontaneity because it is quick-drying and it covers well at the same time. Oil requires waiting because each glaze takes time to dry. It is an exciting technique, creating an opportunity to use a traditional method with a quick-thinking, modern approach. The covering power is visible in this painting in the way the dark, monochrome background becomes a cool, light blue, and also in the way yellow is painted over the very dark brown hair, and over the mauve of the carpet.

The artist changes the shape of the chair to suit the shape of the paper and of the figure. Instead of a rounded back he paints a square, barred back to give strength to the surface pattern of the painting, creating a diverse interest in the slightly slanting angle and its shadow on the wall behind. A sense of the room's space is implied by a line for the junction of wall and floor and the placing of the vase of dried leaves. The carpet pattern provides a delicate yet lively side-interest to the finished painting (10).

10

WOMAN IN A GARDEN
mixed media on paper 21 × 14 inches (53 × 36 cm)

Mixing media is an interesting way of making pictures. Artists have always experimented with combinations of techniques to create a range of effects. Pastels worked into monoprints, and ink and pencil added to watercolors are just two examples. Oil paint, rubbed onto a support with a rag soaked in turpentine, will form a solid color base capable of endless enrichment with pastels, inks or colored pencils. Paper, millboard or stout, sealed cardboard are suitable supports for this kind of work.

The composition of this picture, painted in watercolor and gouache with pencil, ink and pastel elaboration, required thought because of the richness of the available subject matter. Planes were set in relation to the ground level and the table, and the figure was placed in the middle distance behind a large bush which was an atmospheric part of the garden and a contrasting foreground form. The various textures within the picture were of prime concern while working. The mixed media brings out a lively sense of the variety of shape, pattern and color in the garden scene, a variety it would be difficult to suggest in a single medium.

1

5

2

This relaxed, informal view of a woman sitting in a garden poses interesting problems of scale, texture and content. There is a danger, with such busy subjects, that the artist's eye may be overwhelmed and the result be unsatisfactory through attempting to achieve too much. To represent this scene, the artist has to act as a visual editor, selecting areas of prime concern from the mass of detail available. Although the figure is undeniably the main interest in the painting, it is not given a correspondingly prominent position, but assumes its importance through its location. Setting the figure in the middle distance, behind a large, flourishing bush, has the effect of leading the eye back to this point, rather as if the observer is walking down a garden path. The understated, reserved placing of the figure creates a sense of discovery (1).

The initial preparations include stretching the paper, ready for painting in watercolor. A sheet of rough watercolor paper is soaked in water and taped right side up to a board, with gum strip. The two long sides of the paper are taped down first, then the two short sides. Using a large brush charged with pure watercolor, the foliage, table, chair and figure are quickly blocked in.

This initial blocking in of the main forms is loose and suggestive, to allow room for subsequent alteration, while at the same time establishing the main relationships. The chair has shrunk in proportion to its actual size and a soccer ball has been added in the foreground. The ball establishes a ground level in the forefront of the picture and serves to carry the eye back to the figure's face, echoing the shape of the head (2). The watercolor painting is gradually built up, using a variety of shades of green to organize the variety of tones present in the foliage. More detail is added to the figure and a strong vertical established for the wire fence in the background (3). At this stage, the artist introduces a new medium – pen and ink – to add a further dimension to the work. The thin, spidery marks of the pen sharpen up the details and express the spindly stems and pointed leaves of the large foreground plant (4). Taking care to allow the painting to dry before applying the ink, the artist makes quick, light strokes with a dip pen over the painted areas and into the blank spaces (5).

6

7

Further experiment is made with other materials and techniques. Pencil, colored pencil and water-soluble pencil are used to treat some of the background areas of the picture including the fine grid of the wire fence. The tree trunk is drawn boldly with colored pencil. Blots of ink give a depth to the foliage (6). Water-soluble colored pencils are a relatively new medium; combining the fine line possible with pencil with the translucency of watercolor, when water is applied to the drawing. They have many interesting possibilities for the artist. When dampened, the line produced by such a pencil floods the surrounding area with color, but remains visible under the wash (7). White is added to the pure watercolor, making a gouache. This serves to build up the solid areas of color and introduces new tones in the foliage (8).

8

Mixing media is particularly appropriate when there are different textures and different levels of interest to consider in a picture. Simply combining media for the sake of it, or with no thought how the different materials will work together, will not guarantee a sensible result; materials must be chosen with definite effects in mind. Experiment is the best way of becoming aware of the potential of mixed media. In the finished work, the overall impression is one of liveliness, light and movement: this has not been achieved, however, by indiscriminate or haphazard use of media. An element of restraint and a constant awareness of how each addition will combine with the whole are crucial aspects of attempting complex, detailed subjects. Watercolor, gouache, pen and ink, pencil, colored pencil and, in the final stages, oil pastel are all used here; each has its part to play in the rendering of the various textures, tones and forms. Small busy areas are contrasted with large relatively blank spaces; touches of light and color create a vivid surface pattern which suggests movement and vitality. A wide range of colors have been used, including a wide variety of greens, to give depth to the garden landscape (9).

Watercolor

Watercolor painting, a method which has been particularly associated with British artists, is a more recent technique than oil painting, and has been popular since the eighteenth century. It is a difficult technique to master, because the paint is transparent and purists do not use white pigment to produce the lighter tones. Watercolor technique involves the artist working from the lightest through to the darkest tones by laying a series of colored washes. Paintings are usually executed on white paper, the color of the paper itself showing through to provide the light tones. If pure white areas are required, then the paper is left completely uncovered by paint. The pigments, which must be finely ground, are mixed with a water-soluble gum, gum arabic being the most usual. A small amount of added glycerine helps the paint to retain its solubility, even after it has dried.

The best watercolor paper is handmade and has a rough texture which causes tiny points of untouched white paper to sparkle through the washes, giving greater luminosity to the result. It is advisable to stretch watercolor paper before use, to prevent it from buckling and wrinkling as the water soaks in.

Gouache

If white body color is added to the pigment the technique is known as "gouache". The paint used for gouache is not transparent and it is possible to use lighter paint across areas of darker tone. This allows for greater elaboration when painting. It is a less exacting medium than watercolor, but the result is less luminous. An artist wishing to produce spontaneous paintings of figures can choose either of these media, but as watercolor demands a speed of working and its luminous effect implies the changing qualities of light, it seems particularly well suited to capturing the moving figure.

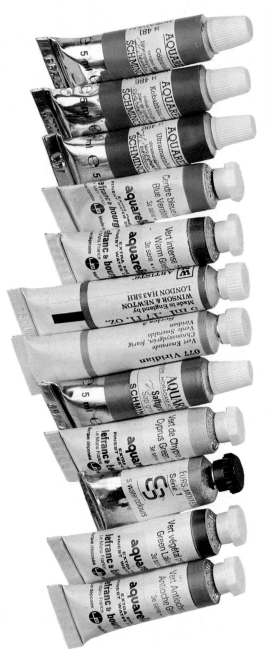

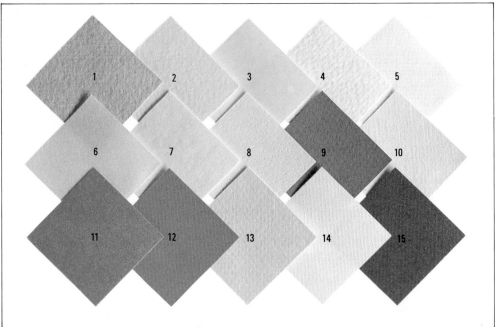

Left Watercolors can be bought in three forms, the most popular being semi-liquid paint in tubes. Semi-moist pans and dry cakes are also available, as are bottles of liquid watercolor with applicators.

Above The range of watercolor papers is almost inexhaustible. Here are just a few: Green's de Wint Rugged (1), Crispbrook handmade (2), Kent (3), Arches M38AM (4), Arches M131AM (5), Rice M11401 (6), Schoellershammer T (7), Schoellershammer (8), Montgolfier (9 and 10), Canson (11), Fabriano (12), Canson Mi Teites (13), and Ingres (14 and 15).

Right *Seated Male by Female on a Couch, both Nude.* In this painting, watercolor has been used and white body added to render the paint opaque. The artist has created strong, shifting light effects in his broad handling of the medium.

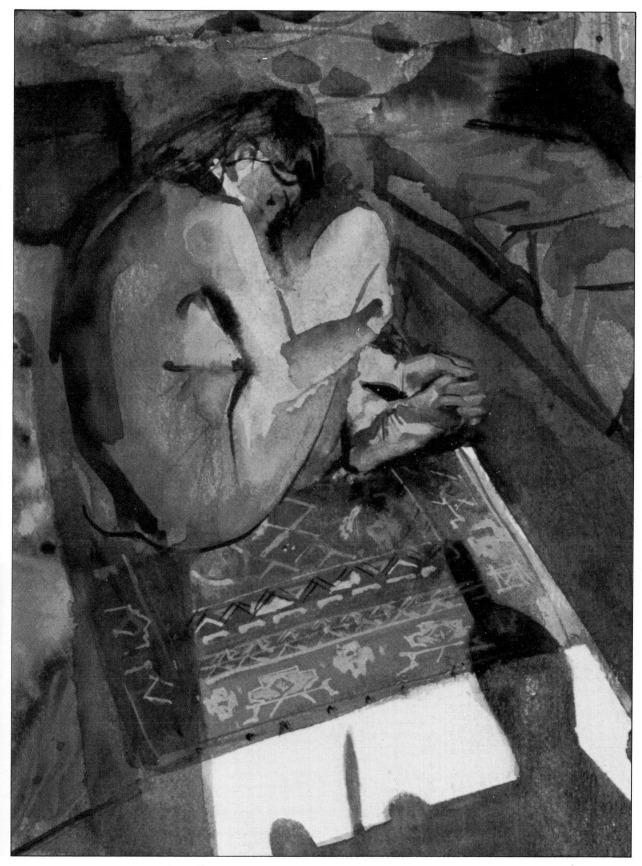

Left *Nude on Oriental Rug.* A true watercolor makes no use of white pigment – or body color – but relies on the white of the paper for the lightest areas in the painting. Such a technique is difficult to master, but it can be particularly effective. This painting includes some small touches of body color in the shadow to the left of the rug and for the restated pattern on the rug itself, but its special quality derives from the large unpainted area in the foreground and the translucency of the washes which depict the figure. The shaft of light from the window creates a border pattern of shadows and slants across the carpet to just touch the side of the huddled figure. The effectiveness of this composition is not only that the diagonal shape of the light area directs the eye to the figure, but that it also draws attention to the woman's vulnerability. A series of warm grey washes suggests the intimacy of the interior.

Acrylics

Recently, the advances in technology have led to the development of a wide range of artificial pigments. Acrylic paints, which are bound in a synthetic resin, are a regular medium with many artists today. They have the advantage of being water-soluble while they are wet but are quick-drying and extremely durable. They are not to be confused with oil paints, however, and cannot be used to achieve such subtle effects, mostly because they are more opaque and do not allow the artist to build up tone and color in the same way.

Brushes and Palette Knives

For all the methods of painting described in this chapter, the most common instrument of application is the brush. Generally the stiffer bristle brushes are used for oil and acrylic painting. A long handle allows the artist to use the brush as an extension of the arm in large, sweeping strokes. For more detailed work and for watercolor, soft sable brushes are a usual choice, but the size, shape and texture of a brush is always a matter of

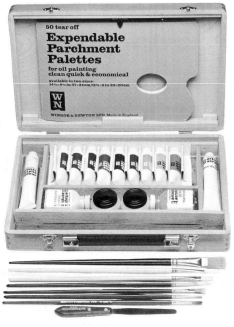

Artist's box
This Winsor and Newton box contains acrylic paints. A plastic emulsion, soluble in water, acrylic allows for thin washes, although not as thin as water-color, as well as thick impasto. Its particular advantages are that it dries very quickly and is permanent.

Left *Girl Sitting on a Bed.* This painting demonstrates the strong colors of acrylic and its covering power. The model is seated on a bed, her back reflected in the mirror. This device is used to extend the picture space and to lighten the background tones. The main color areas are first blocked in with opaque paint, and subsequent layers built up without the colors coming through. The figure is built up in

thin washes and the outlines strengthened with black paint. Lights and darks are contrasted by showing the play of light on the forms.

Above *Beach Scene.* This hot scene illustrates the strong contrasts obtainable from acrylic paints. Constructed from a series of photographs taken from different angles, it demonstrates the "correctability" of the medium: the transparent yellow jacket in the right foreground is a late addition as are the buildings in the background, brought in to close off the picture space and to direct the spectator's eye to the figures. The sense of hazy heat is captured in the shimmery effect of the buildings and blurred outlines of the figures.

individual preference. There is no right or wrong tool for any particular painting technique. Many artists keep a selection of brushes; this would probably include round and flat brushes of varying sizes with handles of different lengths, some made of hog-hair, others of squirrel or sable.

The brush is not the only tool to be used in applying paint; palette knives are also used. Two notable exponents of this technique are Courbet and Vlaminck who painted some of

their pictures entirely with this tool. Palette knives are designed for two distinct purposes: for mixing the paint and for scraping the palette clean. The former are designed in different shapes, usually either spatula- or trowel-shaped. They can be useful in conjunction with a brush for laying in the larger areas of paint. The textural effect given by a palette knife is very different from that of brushstrokes, and it is often considered to be particularly suitable for impasto work.

Sketchbook Preparation

Before embarking on a painting, it is worth being acquainted with some of the basic problems and possibilities inherent in the situation and the composition. By working on a small scale with an implement which lends itself to rapid notation it is possible to discuss the best way to approach the subject, working on angles, lines, tones and even colors until the essence of the desired effect is realized. Sketching works almost like a dialog; suggestions arise, are discussed and then either discarded or accepted.

Some artists work better by "hitting" the support with fervor and directness, allowing the image to emerge spontaneously from a struggle carried out without any preparation. For many, however, the advantages of sketching outweigh the benefits of a spontaneous method of painting. Certain types of work seem to demand a careful and considered approach, and the resulting sense of calm that can be brought into a picture is often important. As a compromise, and to ensure a continuing liveliness while painting, many artists use visual notes only as a general aid, and do not allow themselves to be bound by the lines and spaces, rhythms and intervals of the sketches. The elaborating, changing process continues: angles and stresses may be changed and extraneous elements brought in to increase the atmosphere or add strength.

Above right and right These two sketches offer the viewer intimate glimpses of a girl completely relaxed in her bath. A sense of movement and indulgence is achieved in their combination; separately they may be taken as useful preparatory studies, helping the artist to build up a store of visual information. The back view was established in a very short time, with verticals, including the hose and the girl's spine, creating a symmetry only upset by the glass balanced on a corner. Because the artist is looking down on the girl, a cramped sense of space is implied.
Establishing the idea of a side view, the girl is again sketched briefly but with a little more care. Background details and a mirror reflection are included. The artist still stands above, so that the angles of the side of the bath are sharp, and the body foreshortened.

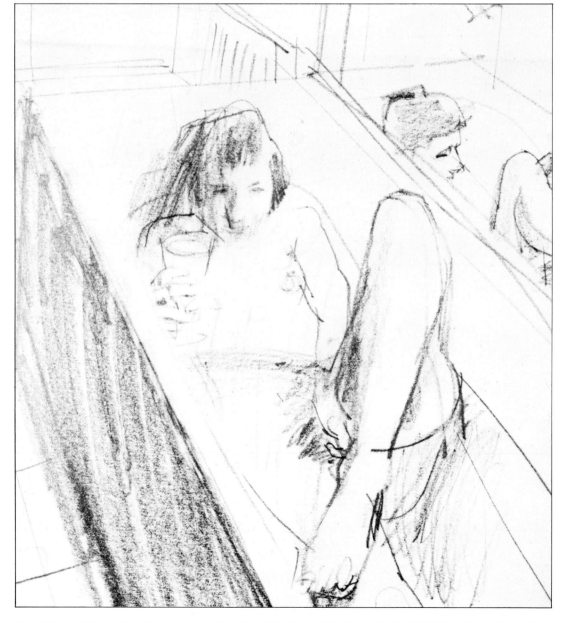

Jellyfish breathe through their skin. Many jellies have skin so thin you can see right through it!

BIG, LITTLE, UPSIDE DOWN!

Thimble jellyfish are one of the smallest species of jellyfish in the world. They grow only to about 1 inch (2.5 cm) wide. These tiny jellies are known for their sting, which can leave swimmers with a red **rash**.

Upside-down jellyfish live in waters near the shore. They lie on the ocean floor upside down. Their moving tentacles look like seaweed. **Algae** live in their tentacles and make their own food using sunlight. Algae share the food they make with the upside-down jellyfish in which they live.

SEA CREATURE FEATURE

Jellyfish were around millions of years before the dinosaurs. Those swimming in Earth's oceans today look very similar to those that lived there long ago.

UPSIDE-DOWN JELLYFISH

The largest species of jellyfish in the world is the lion's mane jellyfish. These jellies can grow up to 8 feet (2.4 m) wide. Their tentacles may be more than 100 feet (30.5 m) long.

A SEA OF LIGHTS

Some species of jellyfish are bioluminescent. This means they can produce light in their bodies. Jellyfish produce light for a number of reasons. Some use light to draw other jellyfish to them when they're ready to have babies.

Since jellyfish are slow swimmers that often just drift along with the ocean, it can be hard for them to catch a meal. Some may use their light to **attract** their **prey**. Once a fish or another small sea creature comes close enough, a jellyfish can eat it.

SEA CREATURE FEATURE

Crystal jellyfish use bioluminescence. They live in the Pacific Ocean along the coast of North America from Alaska to Baja California in Mexico.

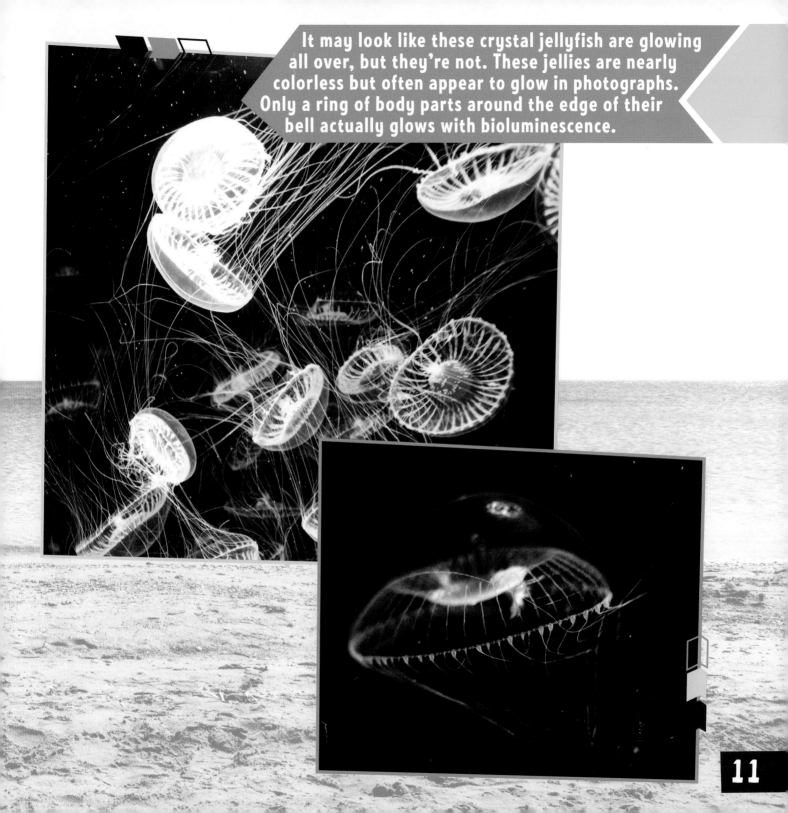

It may look like these crystal jellyfish are glowing all over, but they're not. These jellies are nearly colorless but often appear to glow in photographs. Only a ring of body parts around the edge of their bell actually glows with bioluminescence.

JELLYFISH AROUND THE WORLD

Jellyfish are found around the world. Some species, such as lion's mane jellies, live in cold Arctic waters. Others, such as upside-down jellies, live in warm **tropical** waters. Some jellyfish live along coasts, while others live very deep in the ocean.

Jellyfish often drift where the ocean takes them. When the ocean pulls a huge group together, it's called a bloom. Blooms can be beautiful, but don't get too close if you see one. They're a danger to swimmers. A bloom may contain 100,000 jellyfish!

SEA CREATURE FEATURE

Sometimes jellyfish form blooms themselves. On the darkest night of the month, thousands of box jellyfish come together near the shore in Hawaii to **mate**.

Fried egg jellyfish, such as the one shown here, live in the Mediterranean Sea and the Atlantic Ocean. They're also called Mediterranean jellyfish.

JELLYFISH BLOOM

BABY JELLIES

After mating, a female jellyfish lays thousands of eggs. She carries the eggs for a few days until the larvae inside are ready to **hatch**.

Only a few of the larvae will make it to the ocean floor. There, they fix themselves to rocks or seaweed and turn into **polyps**. As polyps, they grow long stems that end in a ring of tentacles around one mouth. Soon, the top part of the polyp begins to split off. Tiny jellyfish break free and float away.

SEA CREATURE FEATURE

Adult jellyfish are called medusas. Larvae and medusas don't look anything alike.

When a young jellyfish breaks off from a polyp, it's called an ephyra.

DANGEROUS DARTS

To catch their food, jellyfish use special stinging cells called nematocysts. Each nematocyst has a tiny, poisonous dart inside. When a fish brushes against a nematocyst, the tiny dart shoots out. The poison makes the fish unable to swim. Sometimes, it even kills the fish.

A jellyfish may sting with hundreds of its nematocysts. For people, most jellyfish stings are simply painful. However, some jellyfish stings may be deadly. A sting from certain kinds of box jellyfish can kill a person in under 15 minutes.

SEA CREATURE FEATURE

Jellyfish may have nematocysts on their oral arms, tentacles, or mouth.

This black sea nettle has nematocysts on its tentacles, which may grow to be 25 feet (7.6 m) long.

TIME TO EAT

Jellyfish like to eat shrimp, fish, and other small sea animals. Most jellyfish wait for their prey to come to them. Species that feed on larger prey tend to have long tentacles covered with many nematocysts. They sting their prey so it can't swim, then slowly bring it to their mouth through their oral arms.

Some jellyfish eat **plankton**. These jellyfish often have sticky skin and tentacles with tiny hairs. Plankton are pushed past a jellyfish's mouth by the tentacle hairs and become trapped on its sticky skin.

SEA CREATURE FEATURE

Many species of jellyfish will often eat other species of jellyfish!

Jellyfish will eat pretty much anything that crosses their path in the ocean. Jellyfish blooms sometimes cause problems because they don't leave any food for fish to eat!

19

HARMFUL, BUT HELPFUL

A jellyfish's poisonous nematocysts actually help certain other sea creatures. Sea slugs, for example, have a special coating that keeps jellyfish stings from hurting them. This coating lets them keep jellyfish nematocysts on their back and use them to sting other predators.

Jellyfish have a special coating to keep from being stung by their own nematocysts. Tiny fish often swim beneath jellyfish and cover themselves in this coating, which **protects** them from the jellyfish's sting. The fish can then stay under the jellyfish for protection from other predators.

SEA CREATURE FEATURE

Some types of crabs will carry an upside-down jellyfish on their back. The jellyfish hides the crab and protects it by stinging predators that get too close.

Sea turtles love to eat jellyfish. Sadly, they sometimes mistakenly eat trash, such as plastic bags, that looks like jellyfish. Some types of crabs and fish eat jellyfish, too.

PEOPLE AND JELLIES

Jellyfish are high in **protein**, which is something humans need to live. With so many jellyfish in the ocean, some people think jellyfish would be a good food supply for the world's hungry people. In many Asian countries, jellies are a prized food.

Jellyfish are beautiful and interesting animals, but they can be dangerous. To safely look at jellyfish up close, you can visit an aquarium. There, you can view these underwater wonders without worrying about being stung.

GLOSSARY

algae: Living plantlike things that are mostly found in water.

attract: To draw nearer.

hatch: To break open or come out of.

mate: To come together to make babies.

plankton: A tiny plant or animal that floats in the ocean.

polyp: A type of animal with a fixed base, a tubelike body, and a free end with a mouth and tentacles.

prey: An animal hunted by other animals for food.

protect: To keep safe.

protein: A long chain of structural matter made by the body that helps a cell perform major functions.

rash: A group of red spots on the skin.

support: To hold up and help.

tentacle: A long, thin body part that sticks out from an animal's head or mouth.

tropical: Having to do with an area of the world known for warm and wet weather.

INDEX

WEBSITES

Due to the changing nature of Internet links, PowerKids Press has developed an online list of websites related to the subject of this book. This site is updated regularly. Please use this link to access the list: www.powerkidslinks.com/seac/jelly